Make your own Patterns

Make
your
own
Patterns

RENÉ BERGH

NEW
HOLLAND

ACKNOWLEDGEMENTS

I would like to extend my grateful thanks to a number of people: Errol Cornelissen of *Bonwit*, for grading and scaling down my basic patterns on computer; Ruty Tzizik for her support and confidence in my pattern-making skills and for kindly allowing us to photograph some of her garments; Gina Daniel for her beautiful illustrations; Dave Snook for his accurate technical drawings; Clarence Clarke for redrawing the computer patterns; Aage Buus for his patience and lovely photographs; Elaine Levitte for her creative styling; Justine Mallandain and June Sawyer for hair and makeup; Elrika Schreiber for modelling the garments and for her patience, especially with my son Hayden; Kate McCallum for providing the location for the photography; the publishing team consisting of Laura Milton, Janice Evans, Odette Marais, Suzanne Fortescue, Linda de Villiers and especially Susannah Coucher for all their hard work and supportive input; and ultimately to my husband, Neville, for his endless encouragement and support; my sons, Justin and Hayden for their understanding and patience especially during the photo sessions; as well as my mother, Eunice Duffnett, and Liz Newdigate and Myrtle Edwards for looking after my children so that I could work.

First published in the UK in 1995 by
New Holland Publishers (UK) Ltd
Garfield House
86-88 Edgware Road
London W2 2EA
www.newhollandpublishers.com
London • Cape Town • Sydney • Auckland

19 18 17 16 15 14 13 12

ISBN 1 85368 544 5 (hbk)
ISBN 1 85368 702 2 (pbk)

Editor Susannah Coucher
Designer Odette Marais
Assistant designer Suzanne Fortescue
Photographer Aage Buus
Illustrators Gina Daniel and Dave Snook

Typesetting by Struik DTP
Reproduction by Hirt and Carter
Printed and bound in Malaysia by Times Offset (M) Sdn Bhd

Contents

Glossary

Abbreviations:	CF:	Centre front
	CB:	Centre back
	SS:	Side seam
	pc:	Piece (as in 1pc or 2pc collar)

Breakpoint: A point at the centre front edge where the revere starts to fold back.

Ease: An extra measurement that is added to ensure comfort or a looser fit.

Notch: (vb) Cutting wedges from the seam allowances using a notcher.

(n) These symbols are transferred to fabrics to indicate matching points.

Pivot: Support the pattern at a given point, then turn the pattern in a new direction as if on a pivot. This facilitates closing the darts or placing them in another position.

Placket: A garment opening fastened with a zip or buttons.

Revers: Lapel of jacket or blouse which is an extension of the garment front edge.

Roll line: The line from the breakpoint to the shoulder on which the revere folds.

Shift: To move.

Slash: A cut or a slit made in the pattern to facilitate a construction. When slashing, please ensure that you stop cutting just before the end of your mark so that all the pieces still remain attached together. This will guarantee accuracy in further construction.

Square a line: Draw a line at right angles to the given line, using a set square (i.e. at 90 degrees to the given line).

Introduction

M AKE YOUR OWN PATTERNS, with its emphasis on simplicity, is aimed at those who have a basic knowledge of sewing and wish to make their own patterns. Having worked for many years in the rag trade, I discovered that only a certain percentage of people can afford to buy off-the-peg clothes. There are many people who cannot find clothes that fit them properly. Besides, how many of us really have model figures? And then there are those who cannot find styles and colours that suit them, or who simply cannot afford to pay today's prices. Ready-made patterns very often don't fit well either.

I also decided that it was only fair to share some of the secrets that I have learned over the years. These factors inspired me to write this book, resulting in a comprehensive step-by-step guide with easy-to-follow instructions, from basic patterns to innovative styles. As soon as you have furnished yourself with the required tools and equipment, and you have taken your body measurements, you can commence with drafting your basic patterns. No seam allowances have been included in the pattern draft and so need to be added on completion. Three sizes of basic patterns in $\frac{1}{4}$ scale have been included at the end of the book. These patterns also have no seams and may be scaled up as instructed.

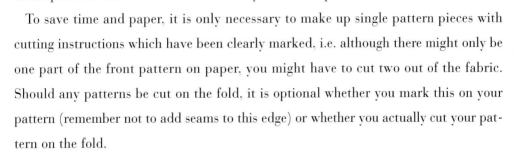

To save time and paper, it is only necessary to make up single pattern pieces with cutting instructions which have been clearly marked, i.e. although there might only be one part of the front pattern on paper, you might have to cut two out of the fabric. Should any patterns be cut on the fold, it is optional whether you mark this on your pattern (remember not to add seams to this edge) or whether you actually cut your pattern on the fold.

Clear instructions with informative illustrations show you how to draft various bodice details, necklines, collars and sleeves, as well as blouses, shirts, basic T-shirts and sweatshirts, jackets, skirts, dresses and trousers. Having fitted your basic patterns, you can now create your own styles by combining details from the various chapters or simply copying your own favourite styles. I hope this book will stimulate your creative ideas. Whatever your situation, whether you plan to make patterns commercially, for your friends or simply for yourself, this is the book for you!

CHAPTER I

Material Requirements

Pattern-making is simpler than it at first appears. It might look technical, but once you have followed the step-by-step instructions, you will soon realize just how easy it is to make your own patterns! When your basic pattern is completed, it is advisable to make it up in calico, or any similar fabric, to ensure that the pattern fits well. Should there be any alterations, they can be rectified on the pattern before drafting any further styles. Experiment first with your pattern-making and soon you will find that with practice your confidence and creative ideas will grow.

Most people will probably make their patterns on the dining room table, but if you're planning a workroom, the ideal height for your table should be about 90 centimetres (3 feet). The size of your table depends on the space you have available – the bigger the table, the greater the work surface.

The next step would be to equip yourself with the necessary tools. Most tools and paper can be bought from stationers or packaging shops, as in the case of pattern cardboard. Industrial sewing machine dealers will stock items such as scissors, pattern notchers, awls, punches and even some metal rulers. When choosing your paper, bear in mind that the firmer the paper, the easier it will be to handle. Soft paper tears easily. Pattern cardboard may be too expensive for everyday use, but it would be advisable, especially for the basic patterns and popular styles. Holes may be punched into the pattern pieces so that each style can be strung together for tidy storage. Another option is to fold pattern pieces neatly and store in large envelopes with descriptions of their contents.

TOOLS REQUIRED

PAPER: FIRM BROWN 'GRIPTIGHT' PAPER OR PATTERN CARDBOARD

SCISSORS: PREFERABLY THE LARGE DRESSMAKING SIZE (ABOUT A 12 CM (4¾ IN) BLADE)

PATTERN NOTCHER

AWL: FOR MARKING DARTS AND POCKETS

RULERS: 30 CM–50 CM (12 IN–18 IN) AND 1 METRE (1 YARD) RULE

PENCILS: 2H AND HB, ERASER

DRESSMAKERS CURVE

PLASTIC SQUARE

PLASTIC FRENCH CURVE

SPIKEY TRACING WHEEL

STAPLER: FOR STAPLING PAPER TOGETHER WHEN CUTTING PATTERNS ON FOLD

STICKY TAPE

TAPE MEASURE

PUNCH: OPTIONAL

Material Requirements

9

CHAPTER II

Body Measurements

It is very important to take accurate body measurements in order to guarantee a good fit to your pattern. You will find that in this chapter we show how and where each relevant measurement is to be taken.

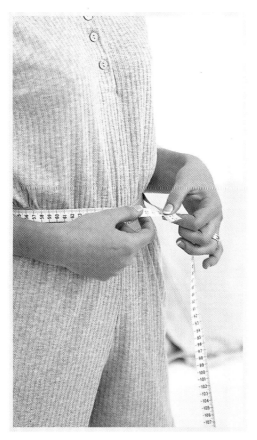

If necessary, ask a friend to take your measurements, taking care to establish the measuring lines indicated overleaf. Please also check your body measurements against those of the measurement chart. If they appear about the same, then use the standard measurements and make slight adjustments at a later stage.

When taking body measurements. wear proper foundation garments (i.e. bra or body suit) with a fairly close-fitting pair of pants (trousers) or skirt and top with a normal sleeve to help you to measure accurately. The measurements should be fairly snug, as they are body measurements. Ease is added at a later stage to facilitate comfort.

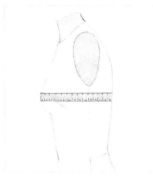

BUST
Around fullest part (about 5 cm (2 in) below the armhole).

WAIST
A fairly snug measurement around the waist.

HIP
Around the fullest part (about 18 cm (7 in) below the waist).

NECK
A fairly loose measurement around the base of the neck.

CENTRE BACK
Measuring from the nape of the neck to the waist.

BACK SHOULDER HEIGHT From the shoulder at the neck to the waist.

CENTRE FRONT
Measuring from the base of the neck to the waist.

FRONT SHOULDER HEIGHT From the shoulder at the neck to the waist.

ACROSS BACK
From armhole to armhole about 12 cm (5 in) down from neck.

FULL BACK
From side seam to side seam about 5 cm (2 in) below armhole.

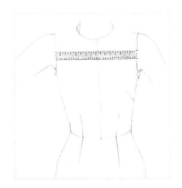

ACROSS FRONT
From armhole to armhole about 7cm (3 in) down from the neck.

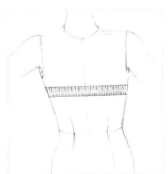

FULL FRONT
Across the bust from side to side about 5 cm (2 in) below armhole.

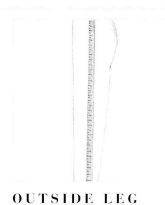

SIDE SEAM
Measuring from the armhole to the waist.

SHOULDER
Measuring from the neck to the sleeve crown.

CROTCH
Taken in a sitting position from the waist to the chair.

OUTSIDE LEG
From the waist over the hip to the ankle.

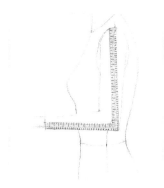

OVERARM
From the sleeve crown around the bent elbow to the wrist.

UNDERARM
From the bottom of the arm-hole to the wrist.

ELBOW
A fairly loose measurement around the bent elbow.

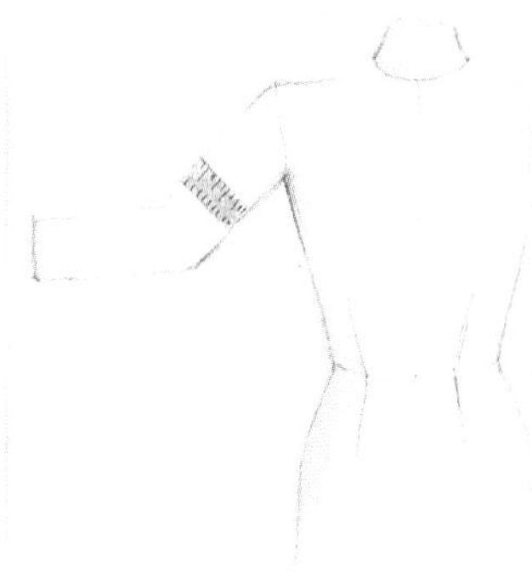

BICEP
Around the fullest part of the upper arm.

THE MEASUREMENTS IN THIS CHART ARE TAKEN FROM AVERAGE BODIES. THE SIZES RANGE FROM 32 TO 46 (10 TO 24). USE THIS AS A GUIDE TO YOUR PARTICULAR SIZE.

SIZES	UK 32 US 10 8		UK 34 US 12 10		UK 36 US 14 12		UK 38 US 16 14		UK 40 US 18 16		UK 42 US 20 18		UK 44 US 22 20		UK 46 US 24 22	
	CM	IN	CM	IN	CM	IN	CM	IN	CM	IN	CM	IN	CM	IN	CM	IN
BUST	82	32	87	34	92	36	97	38	102	40	107	42	112	44	117	46
WAIST	61	24	66	26	71	28	76	30	81	32	86	34	91	36	96	38
HIP	87	34	92	36	97	38	102	40	107	42	112	44	117	46	122	48
NECK	36.5	14½	37.5	15	38.5	15½	40	16	41.5	16½	43	17	44.5	17½	46	18
CENTRE BACK	41.5	16¼	42	16½	42.5	16¾	43.5	17¼	44	17½	45	17¾	45.5	18	46	18
FRONT SHOULDER HEIGHT	42	16½	43.5	17¼	45	17¾	46	18	47.5	18¾	48.5	19¼	50	19¾	51.5	20¼
SHOULDER	12	4¾	12.5	5	13	5¼	13	5¼	13.5	5½	13.5	5½	14	5¾	14.5	5¾
OVERARM	58.5	23	59	23¼	59.5	23½	60	23½	60.5	23¾	61	24	61.5	24¼	62	24½
BICEP	28	11	29	11½	30	12	32	12½	34	13½	36	14¼	38	15	40	16
WRIST	15.5	6	16	6¼	16.5	6½	17.5	6¾	18	7	18.5	7¼	19	7½	19.5	7¾
OUTSIDE LEG	109	43	110	43¼	111	43¾	112	44	113	44½	114	45	115	45¼	116	45¾

Body Measurements

CHAPTER III

Drafting Basic Patterns

In this chapter, the principles and instructions for drafting various basic patterns using standard or individual measurements have been provided. When using standard measurements, you will find that, on completion, the pattern will always be properly balanced. Most people do not have standard-shaped bodies and this is where your own measurements should be used. Owing to the ever-changing fashion silhouettes, these measurements may need to be adjusted from time to time, even though the basic principles of drafting do not change.

THE DRESS BODICE

This construction includes a 5 cm (2 in) ease around the bust and a 2.5 cm (1 in) ease around the waist, allowing for chest expansion and avoiding the ripping of seams. Check that the back and front side seams correspond, as well as your shoulder seams on the back and front, and alter accordingly. The back waist dart may also be altered to correct the waist measurement, if necessary.

THE BACK

SHOULDER HEIGHT

ACROSS BACK

SHOULDER SEAM

CENTRE BACK

FULL BACK

WAISTLINE

SIDE SEAM

STEP 1

AB – Back shoulder height.
Mark this line.

AC – ½ across the back plus 1 cm (³⁄₈ in).
Square the line from A to C.

CD – 5 cm (2 in).
Square the line down from C to D.

STEP 2

DE – Shoulder seam. DE meets AC at E.

BF – Centre back length. Mark F on AB.

EF – Curve this line from E, squaring the neckline at F.

STEP 3

FG – ½ of BF plus 3 cm (1¼ in).

GH – ½ full back measurement plus 1.25 cm (½ in) for ease. Square the line across from G.

FI – ½ FG.

IJ – ½ across back. Square across at I.

GK – Equals IJ.

KL – Draw a diagonal line from K to L to measure 3 cm (1¼ in).

DH – Connect D to J, J to L and L to H to form an armhole.

STEP 4

BM – ¼ waistline plus 4.5 cm (1¾ in) (4 cm or 1½ in for the dart and 0.5 cm or ¼ in for the ease). Square this line.

GN – ½ GK.

BO – GN less 2 cm (¾ in).

OP – 4 cm (1½ in). Join N to O and N to P to form dart.

HQ – Side seam length.
Draw this line from H through M to Q.

QP – Curve Q to P gently to complete the waistline. The back bodice is now ready for any further construction.

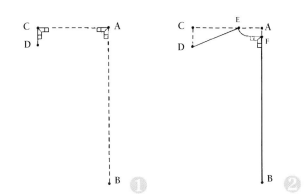

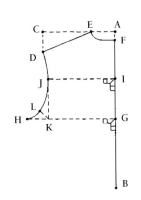

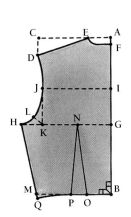

THIS SHIRTWAISTER HAS BEEN BELTED TO FORM A WAISTLINE

To use the back bodice as it is for a dress back, continue with Step 5.

STEP 5

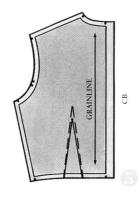

- For a one-piece back, place the centre back on the fold.
- For a zipped back, add a 1.5 cm (⅝ in) seam to the centre back.
- Add 1 cm (⅜ in) seams to all the other edges.
- Shorten the dart by 2.5 cm (1 in) and notch the dart at the waist.
- Notch centre back at the neck and waist and notch shoulder and side seams as indicated.
- These notches will indicate the stitchlines when sewing.
- Double notch the armhole to correspond with the sleeve when the sleeve pattern has been constructed.

THE FRONT

SHOULDER HEIGHT

ACROSS FRONT

SHOULDER SEAM

CENTRE FRONT

FULL FRONT

SIDE SEAM

WAISTLINE

STEP 1

AB – Front shoulder height. Mark this line.

AC – ½ across front plus 1 cm (³⁄₈ in).
Square the line from A to C.

CD – 4 cm (1½ in).
Square the line down from C to D.

STEP 2

DE – Shoulder seam DE meets AC at E.

BF – Centre front length. Mark F on AB.

AG – Equals AE plus 1 cm (³⁄₈ in).
Draw a diagonal line.

EF – Square the line across from F.
Square the line down from ED.
Join E to F through G for a curved neckline.
Reshape after fitting.

STEP 3

BH – Equals ½ AB.

HI – ½ full front measurement plus 1.25 cm (½ in).
Square the line across from H.

FJ – ½ FH.

JK – ½ across the front measurement.
Square across at J.

HL – Equals JK.

LM – Draw a diagonal line from L to M to measure
2.5 cm (1 in).

DI – Connect D to K, K to M and M to I to form
the armhole.

STEP 4

HN – 5 cm (2 in). Mark N on AB.

NO – HI plus 1 cm (³⁄₈ in)

IP – Side seam length. Draw the line from I
through O to P.

NQ – ½ JK plus 1.25 cm (½ in).

BR – NQ less 2 cm (¾ in). Square across at B.

BS – BR plus 4.5 cm (1¾ in).

PS – Join S to P to complete the waistline.

ST – 4.5 cm (1¾ in). Join Q to R and Q to T to
form the dart. The depth of the dart may be
altered to correct the waist measurement, if
necessary. The front bodice is now ready for
further construction. Follow Step 5 for the
addition of a side bust dart and Step 6 for
seam allowances. For a smoother fit over the
bust, it is better to pivot some of the waist
dart to form a side dart as follows:

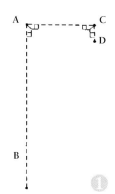

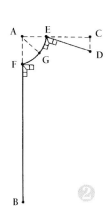

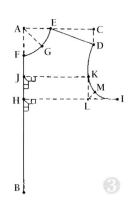

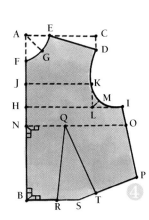

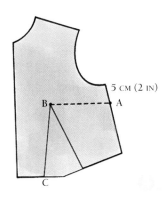

STEP 5

(a) Mark A, 5 cm (2 in) down from the armhole or lower, depending on the position of the bust.

(b) Mark the edge from C to A. Using a pencil at B, pivot the pattern so that the ½ waist dart closes and forms the side dart A to AA.

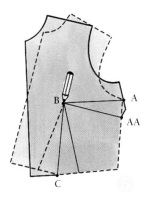

(c) Shorten the dart points by 5 cm (2 in) on the waist and side darts.

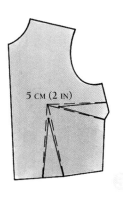

WAIST DARTS GIVE SHAPE TO THIS DRESS BODICE

STEP 6

- Place the centre front line on fold.
- Add 1 cm (³⁄₈ in) seams all round.
- Mark the dart points. Notch the darts at the side and the waist. Always notch the centre front at the neck and the waist. Notch the shoulder and side seams in order to indicate the stitchlines.
- Make a single notch at the armhole to correspond with the sleeve when the sleeve has been constructed.

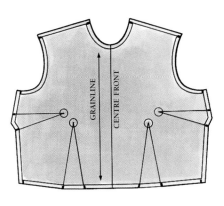

Drafting Basic Patterns

THE SLEEVE

No seam allowance has been included, but it may be added at the completion of this construction. However, an 8 cm (3¼ in) ease at the bicep and a 2.5 cm (1 in) ease at the elbow as well as at the wrist have been included. This will allow for more freedom of movement.

OVERARM

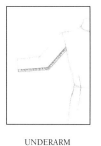

UNDERARM

BICEP

ELBOW

LOOSE WRIST

STEP 1
AB – Overarm length measurement. Mark this line.

BC – Underarm length measurement. Mark C on AB.

AC – Sleeve cap height, about ⅓ of the armhole circumference.

CD – ½ bicep plus a 4 cm (1½ in) ease. Square the line from C.

CE – ½ bicep plus a 4 cm (1½ in) ease. Square the line from C.

STEP 2
BF – ½ BC. Mark F on AB.

FG – ½ the elbow measurement plus 1.25 cm (½ in). Square the line from F.

FH – ½ the elbow measurement plus 1.25 cm (½ in). Square the line from F.

STEP 3
BI – Equals GF minus 2.5 cm (1 in). Square the line from B.

BJ – Equals BI. Square the line from B. Square the line across from A on both sides.

IK – Draw a line from I through G and D to cross the line from A. Mark this point K.

JL – Draw a line from J through H and E to cross the line from A. Mark this point L.

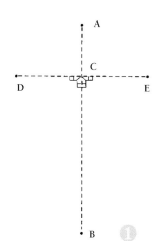

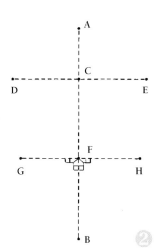

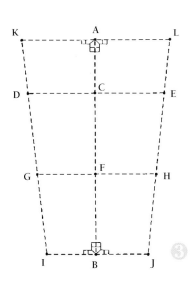

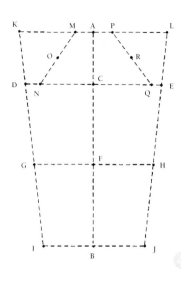

STEP 4

AM – ¼ AK. Mark M on AK.

DN – ¼ DC. Mark N on DC. Join MN.

MO – ½ MN.

Mark O on MN.

AP – ¼ AL. Mark P on AL.

QE – ⅙ CE. Mark Q on CE. Join PQ.

PR – ½ PQ. Mark R on PQ.

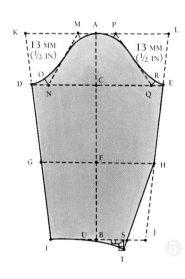

STEP 5

AD – Draw a curved line from A through O to D, shifting M and N about 1.25 cm (½ in) as illustrated. This becomes the front sleeve cap.

AE – Draw a curved line from A through R to E, shifting P and Q about 1.25 cm (½ in) as illustrated.

This becomes the back sleeve cap.

IS – Equals the loose wrist measurement. Mark S on IJ.

ST – 2 cm (¾ in). Square the line down from S.

IU – ½ IB. Mark U on IJ.

IT – Connect I through U to T, thus making sure that the line curves slightly.

TH – Join T to H.

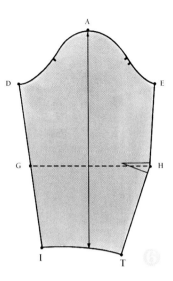

STEP 6

- ET is longer than DI.

- Mark an elbow dart on either side of H, measuring about 9 cm (3½ in) in length and width so that ET (with dart closed) will measure the same as DI. This dart measurement should be ± 3 cm (1¼ in) in width.

- Add 1 cm (⅜ in) seams all round except the hem (IT) which should be about 3 cm (1¼ in) in width. Make one notch in the front cap and two notches in the back cap. Also notch the dart. Mark the grainline from A to B.

- Before notching the centre of the sleeve cap, fit the sleeve onto the back and front bodice armholes. Make the corresponding notches in the front and back armholes.

THIS IS A TYPICAL SET-IN SLEEVE

Drafting Basic Patterns

ALTERING THE SLEEVE CAP OR CROWN

Please check that the basic sleeve fits into the armhole of the bodice pattern which you have used. If not, the following methods may be used to alter the sleeve crown. Please ensure that there is some ease at the top of the crown. The flatter the crown, the less ease is required and likewise, the higher the crown the more ease is required. About a 1 cm (⅜ in) to a 2 cm (¾ in) ease is sufficient.

THIS SLEEVE CROWN HAS BEEN FLATTENED SLIGHTLY

STEP 1
- Draw a line from side seam to side seam at the underarm.
- Draw a line from the centre of the crown perpendicular to the first line.
- Slash a vertical line from the crown downwards and then a horizontal line from the centre to the side seams, ensuring that the parts remain attached.

STEP 2
- For a flatter crown, overlap the panels A and B at the crown as much as is needed.
- Mark the centre of the new crown.

STEP 3
- For a raised crown, lift the panels A and B evenly as necessary and fill in the crown at the centre, making the central notch.
- If the bodice is extended at the side seams, it enlarges the armhole. If a wider sleeve is required, the same measurements may be added to the sleeve side seams from the underarm to the hem.

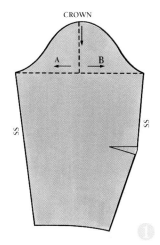

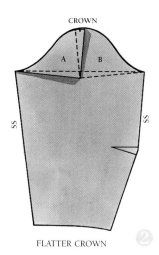

FLATTER CROWN

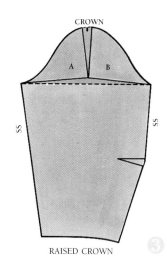

RAISED CROWN

THE JACKET

All jackets require extra ease around the bust, waist, hip, neck and arm so that they may be worn comfortably over blouses or dresses. Use the blouse bodice hip foundation and alter accordingly. For a dartless jacket, alter the dartless shirt pattern (as seen on page 25).

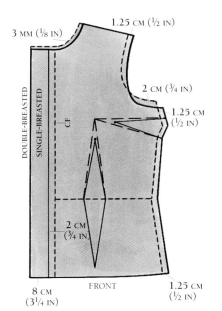

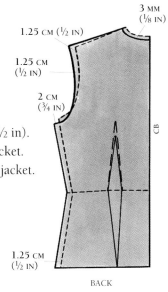

FRONT

Lower neckline by 3 mm (1/8 in).
Extend shoulder by 1.25 cm (1/2 in).
Drop armhole by 2 cm (3/4 in).
Increase bust/hip measurement by 1.25 cm (1/2 in).
Add 2 cm (3/4 in) to CF for single-breasted jacket.
Add 8 cm (3 1/4 in) to CF for double-breasted jacket.

BACK

Lower neckline by 3 mm (1/8 in).
Extend shoulder by 1.25 cm (1/2 in).
Drop armhole by 2 cm (3/4 in).
Increase bust/hip by 1.25 cm (1/2 in).

SLEEVE

Raise crown by 2 cm (3/4 in).
Increase width of crown by 6 mm (1/4 in) on each side.
Widen sleeve at underarm and hem 1.25 cm (1/2 in) on each side.

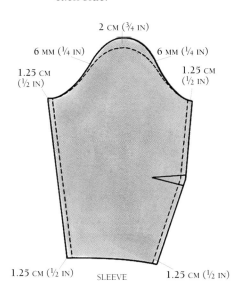

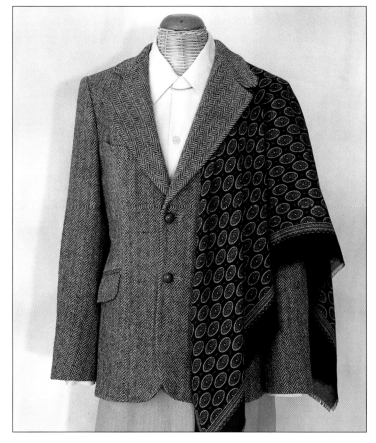

THIS HACKING JACKET IS A GOOD EXAMPLE OF A BASIC FITTED JACKET

THE DARTED BLOUSE

This hip foundation pattern will be quite slim-fitting, because only a 10 cm (4 in) ease has been included around the bust and a 2.5 cm (1 in) ease has been added to the waist.

DARTS ENSURE A SLIM-FITTING, FLATTERING EFFECT

STEP 1

- Using the dress front bodice, pivot at the bust point to make the waist dart about 4 cm (1½ in), enlarging the bust dart.
- Extend the centre front length by 20 cm (8 in).
- Square a line across from C to D to measure that of the bustline at the armhole so that AB equals CD.
- Join to the waist at the side seam, as illustrated.

STEP 2

- Draw a line from the bust point through to the centre of the waist dart to the hem.
- Mark in the balance of the dart below the waist as illustrated.
- Drop the centre front hem by 1 cm (⅜ in), curving the line gently to the side seam.
- Shorten the darts at the bust point by 5 cm (2 in).

STEP 3

- Trace the back bodice.
- Extend the centre back by 20 cm (8 in).
- Square a line across from C to D to measure that of the back bustline AB at the armhole.
- Join to the waist at the side seam, as illustrated.

STEP 4

- Draw a line from the dart point through to the centre of the dart at the waist to the hem.
- Mark in the balance of the dart below the waist as illustrated.
- Shorten the top dart point by 5 cm (2 in).

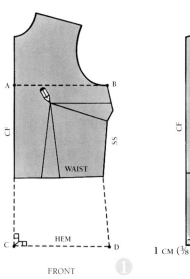

FRONT ❶

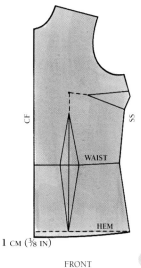

1 CM (⅜ IN)

FRONT ❷

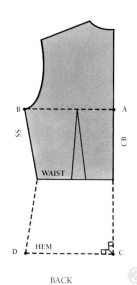

BACK ❸

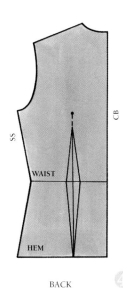

BACK ❹

THE DARTLESS SHIRT

Use the hip foundation pattern to construct a dartless pattern for shirts or blouses. Please note that this pattern can only be used satisfactorily for looser-fitting garments or when using knitted fabrics.

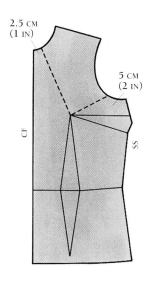
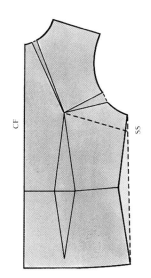
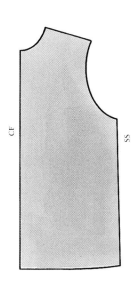

STEP 1
- Mark the position of the slash line on the neck, 2.5 cm (1 in) away from the centre front.
- Draw a line from this point to the bust point.
- Mark the position of the second slash line on the armhole, 5 cm (2 in) away from the side seam.
- Draw a line from this point to the bust point.

STEP 2
- Slash the side dart and these lines from the neck and the armhole respectively, ensuring that the pieces remain attached at the bust point.
- Close the side dart by spreading the neck by 6 mm (¼ in) and leaving the remainder of the spread at the armhole, as illustrated.

STEP 3
- Round off the neck
- Round off the armhole.
- Eliminate the waist darts.
- Straighten the side seam.

- As the armhole increases in size, the same measurement should be added to the sleeve cap, so that the armhole and sleeve correspond.

STEP 4
- Straighten the side seam of the back and eliminate the waist darts.

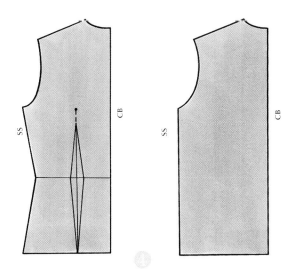

25

THE SKIRT

Skirt lengths and shapes change seasonally, but the basic methods of construction remain the same. The following measurements are required for the skirt construction.

WAIST CIRCUMFERENCE

HIP CIRCUMFERENCE

SWEEP: HEM CIRCUMFERENCE

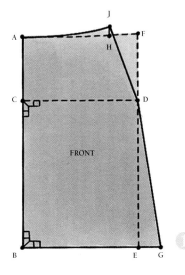

STEP 1

AB – Centre front length.

AC – 16.5 cm (6½ in) down from the waist.

CD – ¼ hip measurement plus a 1.25 cm (½ in) ease.

BE – Equals CD. Square the line from B.

EF – Equals AB plus 6 mm (¼ in). Draw a line from E through D to F.

AF – Connect with a gentle curve.

BG – ¼ sweep. Extend BE to G. Connect G to D.

AH – ¼ waist plus a 1.25 cm (½ in) ease.

HJ – Raise by 1.25 cm (½ in). Curve the line from A to J.

JD – Connect.

STEP 2

BK – Equals ½ BG. Square the line from the side seam to K. Curve the hem gently. Draw the hipline parallel to the hem. An optional 1.25 cm (½ in) dart, 10 cm (4 in) long, may be made at the centre of the waist instead of easing 1.25 cm (½ in) into the waistband.

This ease is necessary in order to accommodate the tucking in of a blouse or a shirt at the waist and also allows for the changes that take place when aligning the waistline.

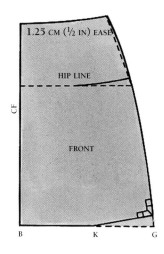

HANDY HINTS

REMEMBER TO ROUND OFF ANY SHARP POINTS, SUCH AS POINT D ON THE HIP LINE, USING YOUR HIP CURVE RULER. TO SOFTEN THE FALL OF THE SKIRT, THE PATTERN MAY BE CUT WITH THE GRAIN ON THE BIAS, AS OPPOSED TO BEING ON THE CENTRE FRONT AND THE CENTRE BACK.

STEP 1

AB – Centre front length plus 1.25 cm (½ in).

AC – 18 cm (7 in) down from the waist.

CD – ¼ hip measurement plus a 1.25 cm (½ in) ease.

BE – Equals CD. Square the line from B.

EF – Equals AB minus 6 mm (¼ in). Draw a line from E through D to F.

AF – Gently curve this line.

BG – ¼ sweep. Extend BE to G. Connect G to D.

CH – 10 cm (4 in) to 11 cm (4¼ in), depending on the size of the hip.

AJ – Equals CH. Connect H to J. Make a V-shaped dart (1.25 cm or ½ in on either side of J).

AK – ¼ waist plus 2.5 cm (1 in) for the dart.

KL – Raise by 1.25 cm (½ in). Curve the line from A through J to L.

LD – Connect.

STEP 2

BM – Equals ½ BG. Square the line from side seam to M, as illustrated. Curve the hem gently. Draw the hipline parallel to the hem. This is purely to indicate the position of the hip.

THE GRAIN OF THIS SKIRT HAS BEEN CUT ON THE BIAS

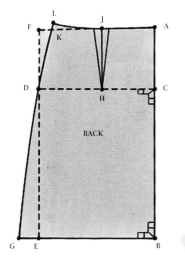

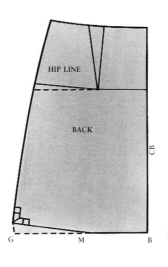

HANDY HINTS

THE LENGTH AND DEPTH OF THE BACK DART MAY VARY, DEPENDING ON THE BODY SHAPE. MULTIPLE DARTS DISTRIBUTE THE FULLNESS ACROSS THE HIP LINE, GIVING ONE A SMOOTHER FIT. ONE USUALLY PLACES THE SECOND DART BETWEEN THE SIDE SEAM AND THE FIRST DART (JH).

Drafting Basic Patterns

TROUSERS

Trousers appear in a variety of lengths from shorts to long trousers. The shape may also vary. but to achieve a good fit, it is necessary to construct your own basic trouser pattern. The measurements below are required for this construction.

WAIST CIRCUMFERENCE

HIP CIRCUMFERENCE

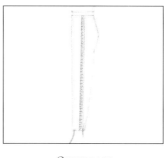

OUTSIDE LEG

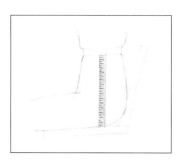

CROTCH DEPTH

STEP 1

AB – Outside leg measurement.

AC – 18 cm (7 in).

CD – ¼ hip measurement plus a 2 cm (¾ in) ease. Square the line from C.

CE – Equals CD. Extend DC to E. Draw arc line above E, pivoting at D.

AF – Crotch depth plus 2.5 cm (1 in) ease. Mark F on AB.

GH – Equals DE. Draw the line through F parallel to DE.

STEP 2

GI – Equals AF minus 1.25 cm (½ in). Square the line up from G.

HJ – ½ FH. Extend GH to J.

HK – ½ HJ.

KL – Equals GI plus 5 cm (2 in). Draw a line from K, touching the outer edge of arc.

GM – Equals KJ.

GN – 4 cm (1½ in). Draw a diagonal line from G. Draw a curved line from D through N to M.

KO – 3 cm (1¼ in). Draw a diagonal line from K. Then draw a curved line from L through O to J.

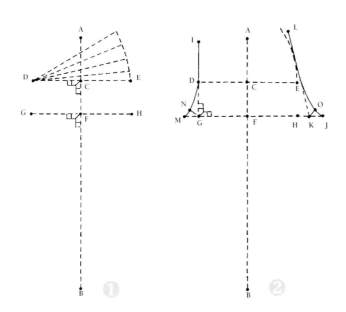

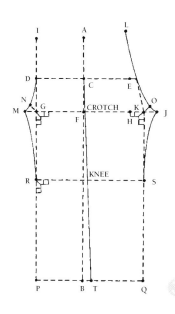

STEP 3

GP – Equals FB. Square the line down from G.

KQ – Equals FB.
Square the line down from K.

PQ – Connect.

PR – ½ PD.

RS – Square the line across from R to S on
KQ. Draw slightly curved lines from M
to R and from J to S.

BT – Equals 2.5 cm (1 in).

TC – Connect.

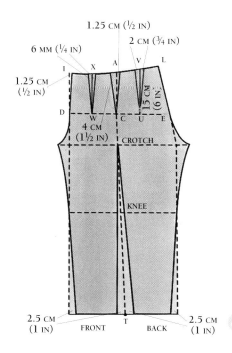

STEP 4

IL – Draw a curved waistline from I through
A to L. Then reduce the waist to fit half of
the waist measurement. First make a part
reduction at the sides and centre front.
Dart the back and front as follows:

CU – ½ CE.

LV – ½ back waist. Make dart 15 cm (6 in) in
length along VU.

DW – ½ DC.

IX – Equals DW. Make a dart from X to W,
about 10 cm (4 in) in length. Reshape the
front and back legs by reducing 2.5 cm
(1 in) on either side of T from the hem
to the crotch line and 2.5 cm (1 in) from
P and Q respectively, to the knee line.
Separate the front and the back. The leg
shape of this pattern is loose. For a slimmer fit, follow the next step.

STEP 5

- Reduce the leg by 2.5 cm (1 in) on each seam
at the knee and 4 cm (1½ in) on each seam at
the hem.
Join from the hem to the knee and then gently curve to the crotch, as illustrated.

- Fold the pattern in half lengthwise, matching
the inside and the outside seams at the hem
and at the knee to establish the grainline.

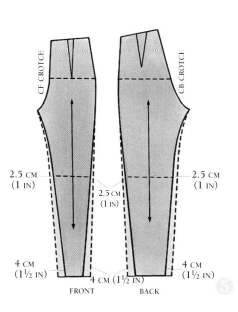

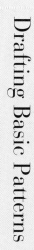

Drafting Basic Patterns

CHAPTER IV

Bodice Details

The details set out in this chapter apply to blouses, shirts, dresses and jackets, even though the constructions shown here have been done using the dress bodice. You may use your basic blouse or basic jacket pattern. The proportions and measurements may vary according to the effect required. The best way of adding fullness to a garment, is to make a yoke with gathers, tucks or pleats. By panelling the garment, a closer fit or slimmer look is achieved. Throughout history, the bodice has always contained a fair amount of detail. Unfortunately we cannot cover every aspect in this book. The details discussed may quite easily be altered using the basic method of construction.

DOUBLE SHOULDER TUCKS

By transferring the bust dart into shoulder tucks, the fit of your basic pattern is maintained. For more fullness, it is necessary to slash the pattern right through from the shoulder to the hem and then spread to the desired width. The amount and depth of the tucks may also then be established.

STEP 1

- Using a bodice with a waist and side dart, mark the position for the tucks 4 cm (1½ in) apart at the shoulder and bust as shown.
- Mark sections A, B and C.

STEP 2

- Slash along the tuck lines and the top edge of the dart, as shown.
- Close the side dart and spread the tucks equally.

STEP 3

- Mark the tuck lines to the desired length, as illustrated.
- The waist dart may be tucked as well, or eased into the waistline.
- Notch the tucks at the shoulder.
- Add the seams.

4 CM (1½ IN)

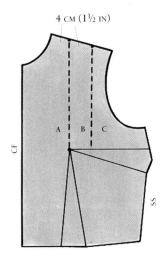

HANDY HINT

WHEN SLASHING, PLEASE ENSURE THAT YOU STOP CUTTING JUST BEFORE THE END OF YOUR MARK SO THAT ALL THE PIECES REMAIN TOGETHER.

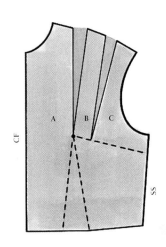

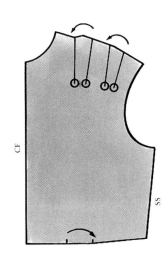

GATHERS AT THE NECK

Once again, the bust dart is transferred into the gathers at the neck. The shape of this neckline may be changed as desired, but should be done before transferring the dart. The centre front of this style looks better when cut on the fold.

STEP 1

- Use the pattern with the waist and side dart.
- Divide the neck into 5 equal sections.
- Divide the armhole into 3 equal sections.
- Join the neck to the armhole marks, the bust and the dart points as indicated.
- Label A to E.

STEP 2

- Slash the dart lines and spreading lines so that all the pieces remain attached.
- Close the waist dart and spread A to B.
- Close the side dart, spreading B to C.
- Spread C to D and D to E, more or less equidistant to that of AB and BC.
- The gathered edge should now measure about 1½ times that of the regular neck.

STEP 3

- Notch the neckline a little away from the shoulder to indicate where the gathers should start and end.
- Add the seams.

HANDY HINTS

WHEN SPREADING THE PATTERN FOR GATHERING, THE GATHERED EDGE SHOULD NORMALLY MEASURE TWICE THAT OF THE EDGE ONTO WHICH IT FITS. FOR EXTRA FULLNESS THE GATHERED EDGE MAY BE INCREASED TO 2½ TIMES OR FOR LESS FULLNESS, ONLY 1½ TIMES THE FITTED MEASUREMENT. THIS NECK CAN BE FINISHED OFF EITHER WITH BINDING OR WITH A TIE.

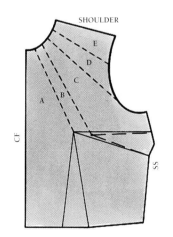

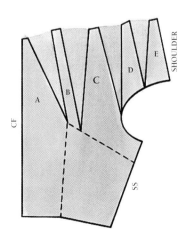

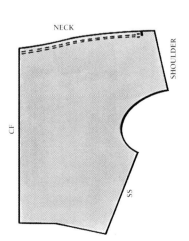

Bodice Details

YOKES

Shapes of yokes can differ extensively from garment to garment. They are quite often cut in contrasting colours or fabric. The bib-shaped yoke described below is frequently associated with a man's dress shirt and is usually pin-tucked throughout. A yoke cut in a checked fabric looks best when placed on the bias.

BIB-SHAPED YOKE

STEP 1
- Establish the position and the shape of the yoke.
- Extend the dart point to coincide with the yoke.
- Shift the waist dart to this point.
- Ensure that this dart remains parallel to the original waist dart.

STEP 2
- Make the crossmark at the bust point.
- Slash through the yoke, separating the yoke from the rest of the bodice.
- Slash the waist dart and half close.
- Slash the side dart and close.

STEP 3
- Make the appropriate notches.
- Cut CF on fold as for this style.
- Add the seams.
- For a button-through shirt, please refer to the separate buttonstand on page 72.

HANDY HINT

BEFORE SEPARATING THE PANELS OR YOKES, ALWAYS REMEMBER TO MAKE A CROSSMARK WHERE THE PANELS MEET SO THAT AFTER SEPARATING AND SPREADING OR CURVING, YOU WILL KNOW EXACTLY WHERE THESE PANELS SHOULD MEET WHEN SEWING.

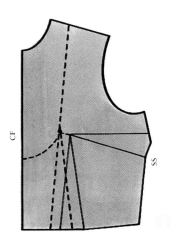

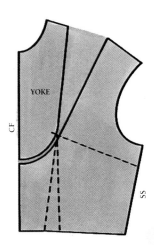

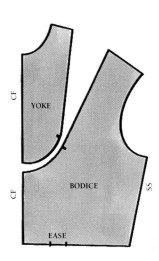

V-CROSSOVER YOKE

This crossover yoke provides one with free movement across the chest. The neckline may be shortened very slightly to avoid gaping. The yoke shape may also be altered, if desired.

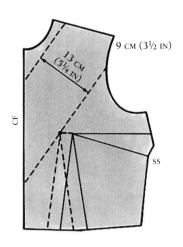

STEP 1

- Extend the dart point by about 6 cm ($2\frac{3}{8}$ in).
- Shift the waist dart to this point.
- Make the armhole mark 9 cm ($3\frac{1}{2}$ in) down from the shoulder.
- Draw a yoke line from this mark, through the new dart point to the centre front.
- Draw the V-neck line parallel to the yoke seam, making the yoke about 13 cm (about $5\frac{1}{4}$ in) wide.

STEP 2

- Make the crossmark at the bust point.
- Slash through the yoke, separating the yoke from the rest of the bodice.
- Slash the waist dart and close half of the dart.
- Slash the side dart and close.

STEP 3

- Place the centre front on the fold of the paper and trace the yoke.
- Open up the paper and extend the neckline to meet the yoke line, as indicated.
- Notch appropriately and add the seams.
- Cut this yoke on the double (i.e. four pieces). Face bodice armhole.

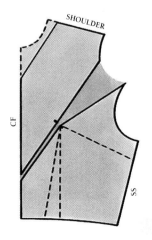

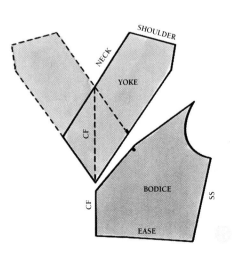

YOKES WITH GATHERS

Gathers falling from the yoke will soften the look of your garment. The dart may be shifted to form gathers. In this way, the original fit is maintained. Slash and spread the bodice for more fullness. Shoulder yokes may be cut on the bias when using checked fabric or on the cross grain when using striped fabric.

SHOULDER YOKES

STEP 1

- Establish the width of the yoke parallel to the shoulder.
- Divide the yoke line into 3 equal parts and connect to the dart point and the parallel point.

STEP 2

- Make the crossmarks on the yoke.
- Slash through the yoke, separating it from the bodice.
- Slash the waist dart, the side dart and the parallel lines, ensuring that all the pieces still remain attached.
- Close half of the waist dart and close the side dart and spread into the parallel lines as shown.

STEP 3

- Notch the crossmarks.
- Notch the corresponding marks to indicate the gathering.
- Add the seams.

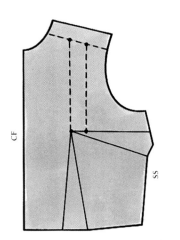

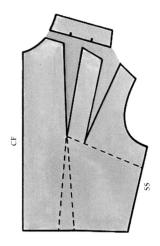

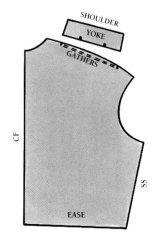

GATHERS MAY BE REPLACED WITH TUCKS AS SHOWN HERE

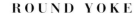

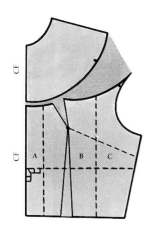

ROUND YOKE

STEP 1

- Establish the depth of the yoke at the centre front.
- Curve the line from this point to the shoulder seam.
- Mark the point about 8 cm (about 3¼ in) from the centre front and connect it to the dart point.

STEP 2

- Make the crossmarks on the yoke.
- Slash through the yoke line, separating the yoke from the bodice.
- Slash the waist dart, the side dart and the line to the yoke.
- Close the side dart completely and the waist dart by half.
- Mark the spreading lines parallel to the centre front, halfway between the centre front and waist dart and halfway between the waist dart and the armhole.
- Mark the working line perpendicular to the centre front.
- Label the panels A, B and C.

STEP 3

- Slash through the spreading lines.
- Draw a second working line.
- Spread the panels A, B and C according to the fullness required, matching the first and second working lines.

STEP 4

- Draw a gentle curve from the centre front to the armhole, trimming off the uneven edge.
- Add the seams and notch the crossmarks to indicate the gathering.

HANDY HINTS

THIS ROUND YOKE IS IDEAL FOR MATERNITY STYLES, ALLOWING PLENTY OF FULLNESS OVER THE BUST AND STOMACH. IT IS ALSO SUITABLE FOR NIGHTIES AND BLOUSES. BEAR IN MIND THAT THE FULLER THE GATHERS ARE, THE SOFTER THE FABRIC SHOULD BE.

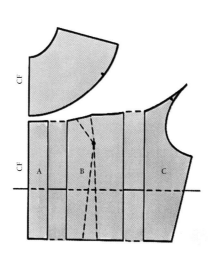

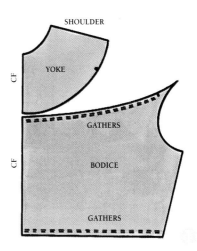

Bodice Details

PANELLING THE BODICE

This line has a slimming effect on the body. Before the advent of stretch fabric, the princess line was often used for swimwear. The panelled bodice first appeared after the Second World War and was incorporated in Dior's 'New Look'.

THE STRAIGHT PRINCESS LINE

The straight princess line is often used in dresses and especially tailored jackets.

STEP 1

- Mark the panel line from the centre of the shoulder to the dart point in both the front and the back.

STEP 3

- Round off the side front panel at the bust slightly and again at the back dart point, to eliminate a sharp point when sewing the garment.
- Add seams and notch the crossmarks.

STEP 2

- Make the crossmarks on either side of the bust point on the front.
- Make a crossmark at the dart point on the back.
- Slash through from the shoulder to the waist on the front and back, cutting out the waist darts.
  Slash the side dart on the front and close.

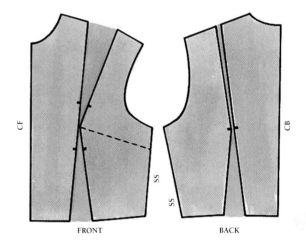

FRONT   BACK

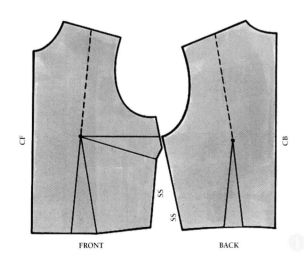

FRONT   BACK

HANDY HINTS

THE PRINCESS LINE IS AN IDEAL SHAPE TO USE FOR FITTED CAMISOLES. FOR A CLOSER FIT, RESHAPE THE PANELS, ESPECIALLY UNDER THE BUST CURVE.

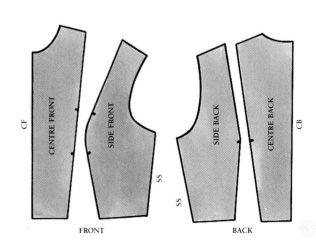

FRONT   BACK

THE CURVED PRINCESS LINE

Although also slimming, this line will accentuate the bust more than the straight princess line.

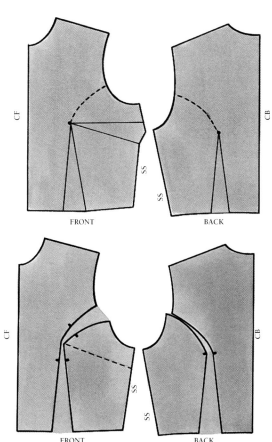

FRONT   BACK

STEP 1

- Mark the panel line about 14 cm (5½ in) down from the shoulder and then draw a curved line to the dart point in both the front and the back sections.

STEP 2

- Make the crossmarks on either side of the bust point on the front and at the dart point on the back.
- Slash through from the armhole to the waist on the front and back, removing the waist darts.
- Slash the side dart on the front and close.

STEP 3

- Round off the side front panel at the bust slightly and also at the back dart point.
- Add seams to all the panels.
- Notch the crossmarks and other appropriate places.

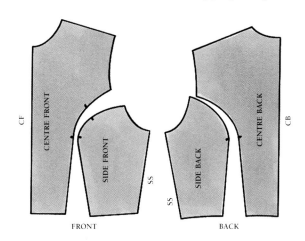

FRONT   BACK

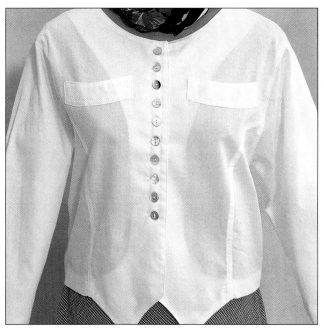

HERE IS AN EXAMPLE OF A LOOSE-FITTING PRINCESS LINE

Bodice Details

Necklines

The focal point of all garments is the neckline. Measurements used for any detail added to the neck. such as collars or ties. should be carefully decided upon so that they remain in proportion to the rest of the style. The Elizabethan ruff of starched lace was popular in the early 1600s. followed by the large lace-trimmed Vandyke collar. Necklines plunged during the time of Napoleon. Off-the-shoulder necklines started appearing in the mid-1850s. By the start of the 20th century. necklines shot up to virtually below the chin. Today anything goes!

These three necklines slip easily over the head and therefore do not require any further opening such as buttons or zips. This will, however, depend on the fit of the rest of the garment. The deep scoop neck is mostly used for vest styles.

BOAT NECK

- Mark the boat neck about 5 cm (2 in) away from the armhole or as desired.
- Curve this line to meet at the centre front neck.

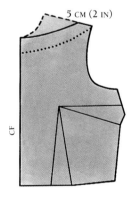

V-NECK

- Mark the V-neck ±3 cm (1¼ in) away from the neck and ±13 cm (± 5¼ in) down from centre front neck. This line should be slightly curved for a better shape.
- All scooped necklines should be reduced for a closer fit.

DEEP SCOOP NECK

- Mark the scoop neck about 5 cm (2 in) away from the neck and about 13 cm (about 5¼ in) down from the centre front neck.
- Reduce the neckline at the centre front by 1 cm (³⁄₈ in) to avoid gaping. For a sleeveless armhole, mark the shoulder 2 cm (³⁄₄ in) narrower at the armhole. Reduce the armhole by 1 cm (³⁄₈ in) and raise the armhole by 2 cm (³⁄₄ in) as indicated.

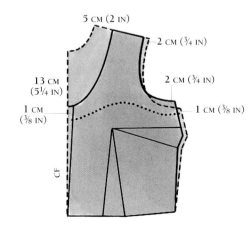

FACINGS

THESE ARE MADE PARALLEL TO THE NECKLINES AND USUALLY FINISH BETWEEN 4 CM – 6 CM (1½ IN – 2³⁄₈ IN) IN WIDTH. THE ARMHOLE AND NECK FACINGS MAY BE CUT IN ONE AS INDICATED ABOVE. ALTERNATIVELY, THESE EDGES MAY BE BOUND WITH THE FABRIC CUT ON THE BIAS ABOUT 3 CM (1¼ IN) WIDE.

CROSSOVER NECKLINE WITH TUCKS

This construction works well for a wrap top, preferably made from a knitted fabric. Simply add ties to the tucked side seam and an opening in the right-hand side seam through which to thread the tie.

STEP 1

- Mark left and right bodices, reducing centre front by 1 cm (⅜ in) on either side.
- Mark the curved neckline 3 cm (1¼ in) away from the neck to the mark at the side seam about 8 cm (3¼ in) above the waist.

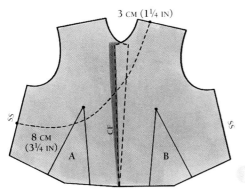

STEP 2

- Cut out the front with the new neckline.
- Slash dart A and close.
- Trim the neckline.
- Divide the 8 cm (3¼ in) side seam into 4 parts (2 cm or ¾ in apart)
- Divide the side of dart B into 3 parts as indicated.
- Join these marks for slashing.

STEP 3

- Cut out dart B.
- Slash the lines so that all the pieces still remain attached at the base of the dart.
- Spread evenly as shown in the illustration.
- Close dart B.

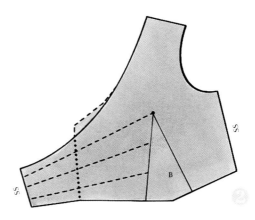

STEP 4

- Mark the grain, preferably on the bias for a better fit.
- Add the seams all around.
- Notch the tucks accurately.

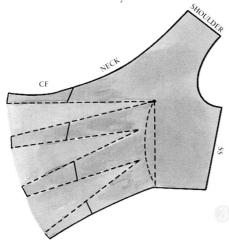

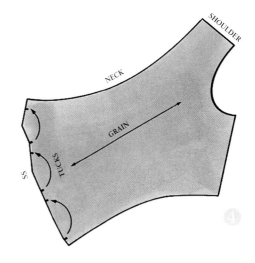

COWL WITH A TRIPLE DRAPE

In order to achieve the soft draping effect of a cowl neck, it is necessary to use a knitted fabric or a woven material which is supple enough to drape.

STEP 1

- Mark the V-neck 10 cm (4 in) down from the centre front and 2.5 cm (1 in) away from the neck at the shoulder.
- For panel A, mark a slightly curved line from the V-neck to the mark 2.5 cm (1 in) away from the V-neck at the shoulder.
- For panel B, mark the curved line 2.5 cm (1 in) down from the V-neck to the shoulder at the armhole.
- For panel C, mark the curve line 2.5 cm (1 in) down from panel B at the centre front to the half mark on the armhole.

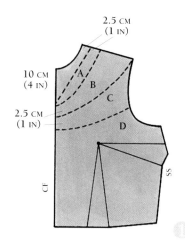

STEP 2

- Cut out the V-neck.
- Slash the lines from the centre front to the shoulder and the armholes so that A to D are still attached.
- Draw the squared lines and spread A to D (to allow for drapes), ensuring that the sections A to D touch the squared line as illustrated.
- The centre front needs to be extended by about 6 mm (¼ in) so that the hem is squared with the centre front.

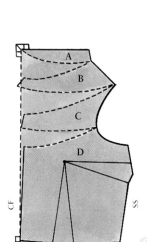

STEP 3

- Reduce the length of the darts by about 5 cm (2 in).
- Add a 2.5 cm (1 in) hem to the neck.
- Add 1 cm (⅜ in) seams.
- Notch the darts. Mark the grainline on the bias.

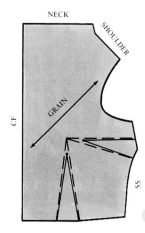

HANDY HINTS

THE CENTRE FRONT SHOULD ALWAYS BE CUT ON THE FOLD AND THE GRAINLINE SHOULD ALWAYS BE ON THE BIAS TO ENSURE THE BEST RESULTS. IDEALLY, ONE SHOULD USE THE DARTLESS BLOUSE PATTERN FOR THIS STYLE. IF SO, STEP 3 CAN BE OMITTED. FOR DEEPER DRAPES, TUCKS MAY BE ADDED TO THE SHOULDER SEAM. BY STITCHING TUCKS DOWN ABOUT 6 CM (2⅜ IN), A PLEATED COWL WILL RESULT.

NARROW TIE

CB

SHOULDER

CF

65 CM (25½ IN)

CUT 2

- This tie looks best made with a firm fabric rather than a very soft one.
- Measure the neck from the centre back to the centre front.
- Then add about 65 cm (25½ in) to this measurement for the length of the tie.
- Mark the width about 6 cm (2⅜ in).
- Add the seams and notch the shoulder seam and centre front.
- This tie has a centre back seam and folds over to finish 3 cm (±1¼ in) wide.
- Cut 2 pieces.

NOTE

BECAUSE OF ITS CURVED SHAPE, THE JABOT IS CONSTRUCTED ON THE FOLD.

WIDE TIE

CB

SHOULDER

CF

75 CM (29½ IN)

65 CM (25½ IN)

CUT 2

6 CM (2⅜ IN)

- Soft, flowing fabric would be ideally suited to this type of tie.
- Measure the neck from the centre back to the centre front. Add about 75 cm (29½ in) to this measurement.
- Mark the width about 16 cm (6¼ in).
- Fold the width in half to cut a diagonal at one end so that the shorter length measures about 65 cm (25½ in).
- Add the seams and notch the shoulder seam and centre front.
- This wide tie is best cut on the bias, but it can also be cut on the straight grain.
- There is a centre back seam and the tie folds over to finish 8 cm (about 3¼ in) wide.
- Cut 2 pieces.

JABOT

4 CM (1½ IN)

SHOULDER

CF

30 CM (11¾ IN)

CUT 4

10 CM (4 IN)

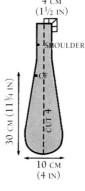

- A jabot is a tie-cum-ruffle worn down the front of a bodice and fastened at the neck, as illustrated. They look attractive when trimmed with lace edging or even when cut entirely out of lace. Frills may also be added across the jabot for an interesting baroque look.
- Fold the paper in half lengthwise. Measure the neck from the centre back to the centre front.
- Add 30 cm (11¾ in) to this measurement.
- Mark the width from 2 cm (¾ in) at the centre back to 5 cm (2 in) at the further end. Curve this line gently and round off the wider end.
- Unfold the paper to reveal the true shape. Add the seams and notch the shoulder seam and centre front on one side only.
- This tie allows for a centre back seam.
- Cut 4 pieces.

Necklines

GATHERED FRILL

Gathered frills at the neck are very feminine, especially when using soft, flowing fabric or lace. The widths of the frills may vary and may even be trimmed with lace edging.

STEP 3

- Establish the width of the frill.
- Measure the neck from the centre front to the centre back (i.e. ½ neck measurement).
- Double that measurement for the length of ½ frill.
- Add the seams.

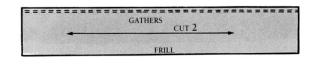

GATHERS
CUT 2
FRILL

SEWING

- Gather the frill evenly.
- Match the centre front seam of the frill to the centre front notch on the bodice.
- Do not join the centre back seam of the frill but match to the centre back zip.
- After attaching the frill to the bodice, bind the neck edge to cover the raw edges of the fabric.

STEP 1

- Establish the shape of the front neck and cut it out.
- If the neck is deep and wide, reduce the neck by 1 cm (⅜ in) on either side of the centre front.
- Shorten the darts by 5 cm (2 in).
- Add the seams and notch the darts, the centre front and the shoulder seams.

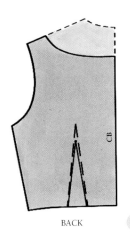

FRONT

STEP 2

- Establish the shape of the back neck so that the shoulder widths match.
- Shorten the dart by 5 cm (2 in).
- Add a 1.5 cm (⅝ in) seam to the centre back for the zip and for the rest add 1 cm (⅜ in).
- Make appropriate notches.

BACK

HANDY HINT

WHEN ESTABLISHING THE FULLNESS OF A FRILL, BEAR IN MIND THAT THE SOFTER THE FABRIC, THE FULLER THE FRILL MUST BE.

GATHERED FRILLS MAY ALSO BE USED ON V-NECKS AS SHOWN ABOVE

FLARED FRILL

Depending on the effect one wants to achieve, a crisp organza or a soft voile may be used. Various widths of frills, layered and attached at the neck, can create a carnival appearance.

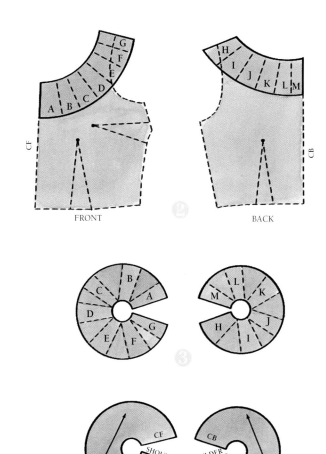

STEP 1

- For the back and front bodice, follow the same method as for the gathered frill style.

STEP 2

- Establish the width of the frill for the front and back necklines alike.
- Extend the shoulders, if necessary, and curve the lines parallel to the necklines.
- Divide the front into 7 equal sections and mark each section from A to G.
- Divide the back into 6 equal sections and mark them H to M, as illustrated.

STEP 3

- Cut out the back and front frill.
- Slash towards the neck, ensuring that all the pieces remain attached.
- Spread the sections to form a circle, leaving a 2 cm (¾ in) gap between the front shoulder and centre front and the back shoulder and centre back. This allows for seams to be added.

STEP 4

- Add a 1 cm (⅜ in) seam all round, except for the hem which should be as narrow as possible because of its circular curve.
- The centre front and centre back seams are best cut on the bias.
- Mark the grain accordingly.
- Finish the neck with binding.

HANDY HINTS

HEMMING FLARED FRILLS CAN BE TRICKY BECAUSE ROPING OR TWISTING OFTEN OCCURS. THERE ARE VARIOUS WAYS OF OVER-COMING THIS. BINDING THE EDGE WORKS WELL; ROLLING THE HEM AND HANDSTITCHING IS TIME-CONSUMING BUT VERY EFFEC-TIVE; ATTACHING A LACE EDGING OR EVEN MACHINING A VERY NARROW HEM IS ALSO ACCEPTABLE. ANOTHER ALTERNATIVE IS TO FACE THE FRILL IN A CONTRASTING COLOUR USING THE SAME PATTERNS. THERE ARE QUITE A FEW OPTIONS.

Necklines

OFF THE SHOULDER

Décolleté necklines are appealing. They may have frills attached, as in the style discussed here. They may have thin straps attached or may be strapless. This styling is particularly suited for the slimmer figure.

STEP 1

- Trace the outline of the front and the back bodices.
- On the front, drop the neckline about 13 cm (about 5¼ in) and reduce the neckline by 1 cm (⅜ in) at the centre front.
- For a sleeveless armhole, reduce the armhole by 1 cm (⅜ in) and raise by 2 cm (¾ in) on the front and back.
- Join the centre front to the armhole (this line may be slightly curved or straight, depending on the centre front height).
- Join the armhole to the centre back, marking the line perpendicular to the centre back.
- Mark the centre of the shoulder to the bust point in the front and the dart point at the back.
- Mark the straps to finish 3 cm (1¼ in) wide.
- Shorten the darts by 5 cm (2 in).

STEP 2

- Cut out the straps and join at the shoulder.
- Add the seams all round.
- Make one notch to indicate the front and two notches to indicate the back of the strap.
- Cut the centre front on the fold and mark the grain.
- Add a 1.5 cm (⅝ in) seam to the centre back and 1 cm (⅜ in) to the remaining edges.
- Notch the dart and the strap positions.
- Make the facings for the front and back about 5 cm (2 in) wide and add the seams.

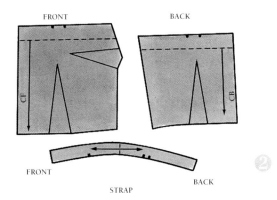

STEP 3

- Establish the width of the frill.
- Measure the centre front to the strap notch, the centre back to the strap notch and the strap length.
- Add these three measurements together and double or increase by 2½ to 3 times, depending on the fullness required.
- Add the seams and notch the gathering line. Keep the hems narrow.

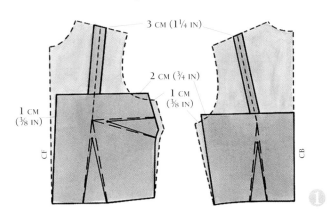

SEWING

- Gather the frill evenly and attach to the bodice between the front straps and the back straps.
- Elasticate the frill around the arm from strap to strap to allow one to wear it off the shoulder or on the shoulder, as illustrated above.

WIDE V-NECK

- Establish the shape of the neckline and the width of the frill.
- Measure the neckline and multiply that measurement by 2, 2½ or 3 times, depending on the fullness required for the frill.
- This frill can also be made with a centre back seam to save fabric.

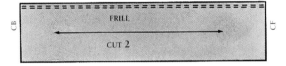

GATHERS

CB / FRILL / CUT 2 / CF

CROSSOVER

- Establish the shape of the neck for the crossover, and the width of the frill at the centre back. Measure the neck from the centre back over the shoulder to the side front seam.
- Multiply that measurement by 2, 2½ or 3 times, depending on the fullness required.
- Maintain the width of the frill from the centre back for two-thirds of the way, then gently curve to nothing at the side seam.

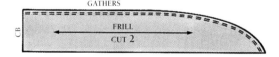

GATHERS

CB / FRILL / CUT 2

HIGH NECK

- This frill should be cut on the fold lengthwise for extra body to enable the frill to stand up.
- Establish the position of the frill at the buttonstand and measure from this point around the neck to the centre front on the opposite front.
- Multiply this measurement by 2.
- Establish width at centre back and double this measurement.
- Curve gently to nothing at both ends.
- Face the neck and buttonstand.
- Cut the frill on the bias or the straight grain.

CF / FRILL / CUT 1 / GATHERS / GATHERS / CF

Necklines

HALTER NECK

The halter neck is a band attached at the front and running around the neck. In this way a backless effect is created.

STEP 1

- Trace the outline of the front and back bodice.
- On the front, drop the neckline by about 13 cm (about 5¼ in), reducing the neckline by 1 cm (⅜ in) at the centre front.
- Curve this line from the centre front to the neck at the shoulder.
- Mark the shoulder 5 cm (2 in) wide.
- For a sleeveless armhole, reduce the armhole by 1 cm (⅜ in) and raise it by 2 cm (¾ in) on the front and back.
- Curve this line from the armhole to the shoulder on the front.
- Join the back armhole to the centre back so that this line is perpendicular to the centre back.
- Mark the back neck band 5 cm (2 in) wide at the shoulder and centre back. Curve this line parallel to the back neck. Depending on the fabric used, this band may need to be suppressed on the outside curve.

STEP 2

- Cut out the back neck band and join onto the front neck at the shoulder, thereby extending the neck strap. Shorten the bust dart by 5 cm (2 in).
- Eliminate the waist darts and ease instead.
- Cut the centre front on the fold.
- Add 3 cm (about 1¼ in) to the length of the neck band on the right-hand side only, to allow for a button to be stitched on.
- Add 1 cm (⅜ in) seams all round except for the centre back bodice which should be 1.5 cm (⅝ in) in order to allow for a zip.

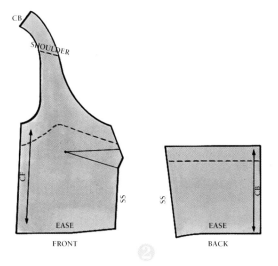

STEP 3

- Cut the back facing 5 cm (2 in) wide.
- Add the seams.
- Cut front facing 5 cm (2 in) wide at centre front and 5 cm (2 in) wide at armhole.
- Curve line as indicated.
- Add the seams and cut the centre front on the fold.

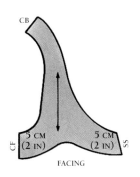

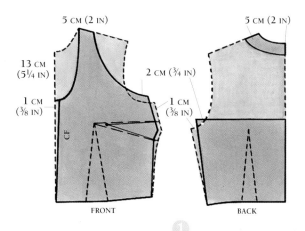

COLLARS

Collars fall into three main categories, the flat-fitting, the rolled and the stand-up. The flat-fitting collar, regardless of width, rolls over from the neckline seam and either ripples or lies flat. The rolled collar, again regardless of width, is a collar that has a collarstand.

PETER PAN COLLAR

STEP 1
- Trace the back and front bodice so that shoulder seams overlap at armhole by 1 cm ($\frac{3}{8}$ in) as illustrated. This forms a 3 mm ($\frac{1}{8}$ in) roll, concealing the neck seam.
- Drop the front neck by 1 cm ($\frac{3}{8}$ in) to nothing at the shoulder.

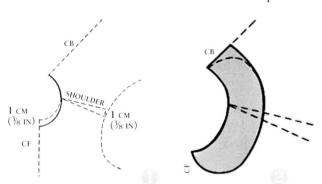

STEP 2
- Establish the width of the collar at the back of the neck.
- Draw the outer edge of the collar parallel to the neckline, curving at the centre front.
- Cut the centre back on the fold and add 1 cm ($\frac{3}{8}$ in) seams all round.
- Notch the collar at the shoulder and at the centre back.
- Cut twice for the top and underside of the collar.

SAILOR COLLAR

STEP 1
- Overlap the shoulder seams by 1 cm ($\frac{3}{8}$ in) as for the Peter Pan collar.
- Establish the depth of the V-neck at the centre front and connect to the neck at the shoulder.
- Establish the depth of the collar at CB.
- Square this line.
- Establish the width of collar.
- Connect the width of the collar to the V-neck at the centre front.
- Cut the centre back on the fold.
- Add 1 cm ($\frac{3}{8}$ in) seams all round.
- Notch the collar at the centre back and at the shoulder.
- Cut twice for the top and underside of the collar.

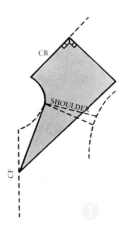

HANDY HINT

THE CENTRE BACK OF THE PETER PAN COLLAR MAY ALSO BE CURVED IF A BACK OPENING IS DESIRED (CUT 4 TIMES).

Necklines

ONE-PIECE SHIRT COLLAR

The average one-piece collar measures between 6 cm (2⅜ in) and 9 cm (3½ in) at the centre back. A wider collar will form a higher stand.

STEP 1

- Drop the centre front neck on the bodice by 1 cm (⅜ in).
- Measure the new neckline from the centre back to the centre front.
- Establish the centre back width of the collar.
- Draw a rectangle using these measurements.

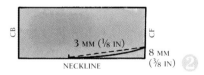

STEP 2

- Measure the centre back to the shoulder and crossmark.
- At the centre front measure up 8 mm (almost ⅜ in) and crossmark.
- Join these two crossmarks with a dotted line.
- Drop the centre of the dotted line by 3 mm (⅛ in) and draw a curved line from the shoulder crossmark to the centre front as illustrated.

STEP 3

- For a pointed collar, extend the collar line by the same amount as the width at the centre front.
- The collar point will depend on the shape desired.
- Cut the centre back on the fold and add 1 cm (⅜ in) seams all round.
- Notch the collar at the centre back and at the shoulder.
- Cut two pieces (i.e. for the top and underside of the collar).

MANDARIN COLLAR

To ensure more ease at the neck, drop the centre front on the bodice by 1 cm (³⁄₈ in).

AB – Centre back of the collar.
Draw a vertical line of 3 cm (about 1¼ in).

AC – ½ neck circumference minus 1 cm (³⁄₈ in).
Square this line from A.

AD – 4 cm (about 1½ in).

CE – 5 cm (2 in). Square this line from C.

DE – Join with the dotted line. Then curve DE by dropping the dotted line 1 cm (³⁄₈ in) about halfway between D and E as illustrated.

EF – 3 cm (about 1¼ in). Square this line from E.

BF – Join, maintaining a 3 cm (about 1¼ in) width and keeping the line parallel to AE.

BFE may be squared at the centre front or curved, as desired. Cut the centre back on the fold and add 1 cm (³⁄₈ in) seams all round. Notch the collar at the centre back and at the shoulder. Cut two pieces (i.e. one for the top and one for the underside of the collar).

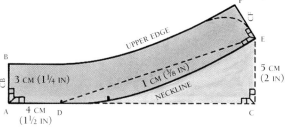

TWO-PIECE SHIRT COLLAR

COLLARSTAND

- Follow the instructions given above.
- Extend AE and BF by 1.5 cm (⁵⁄₈ in) to allow for the button and buttonhole.
- Cut centre back on fold and add 1 cm (³⁄₈ in) seams all round.
- Notch the shoulder, the seam allowance and A, B and F.
- Cut two collarstands – one each for underside and top.

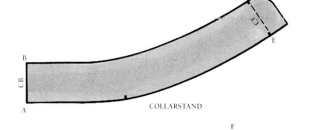

COLLARSTAND

COLLAR

- Follow the instructions for the mandarin collar. Extend AB by 2 cm (¾ in) and FE by 4 cm (about 1½ in).
- Drop F by 1 cm (³⁄₈ in) and curve the line to join A as illustrated.
- Cut CB on the fold and add 1 cm (³⁄₈ in) seams all round, notching centre back at A and new F at centre front.
- Variations can be made to the collar point as indicated 1, 2, 3. Cut two – one for the top collar and one for the underside of the collar.

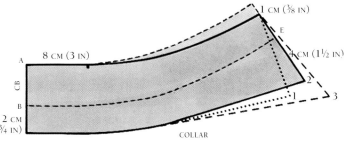

COLLAR

Necklines

NOTCHED COLLAR

The notched collar is made up of a collar with a separate revers or lapel. It is more frequently used for jacket constructions. These instructions are easier than they at first appear and should be followed very carefully to ensure accuracy.

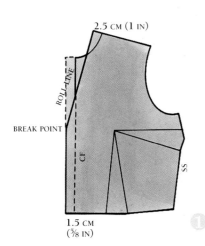

STEP 1

- Trace the front bodice.
- Extend the shoulder towards the neck by 2.5 cm (1 in) for the collarstand.
- Add 1.5 cm (⅝ in) to the centre front for the buttonstand.
- Draw a parallel line.
- Establish the break point on this line and connect it to the extended shoulder as illustrated. This line becomes the roll line.

STEP 2

- Fold the paper under along the roll line.
- Using the tracing wheel, trace through the neckline and the collarstand.

STEP 3

- Unfold the paper and pencil in perforated lines.
- From the neckline intersection A, draw the desired revere ending at the breakpoint, as illustrated.
- Divide the neckline AB in half and mark at C.
- Extend B by 6 mm (¼ in) and mark this point D. This allows more ease to the outside edge of the collar.

HANDY HINT

IT IS NOT NECESSARY TO HAVE A BACK NECK FACING, AS THE TOP COLLAR COVERS THE BACK NECK SEAM. HOWEVER, IF A FACING IS DESIRED, ENSURE THAT THE SHOULDER MEASUREMENTS OF THE FACINGS CORRESPOND.

2.5 CM (1 IN)

ROLL LINE

BREAK POINT

CF

SS

1.5 CM (⅝ IN)

①

COLLARSTAND

NECKLINE

CF

SS

②

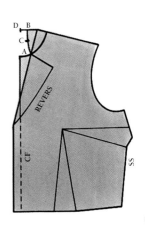

D B
C
A

REVERS

CF

SS

③

STEP 4

- Draw a straight line from C through D to E so that DE equals the back neck measurement.
- Square a line from E to F measuring about 7 cm (2¾ in).
- Square a line from F to the shoulder and draw the desired shape of the collar, finishing at the top revere line.
- Mark this intersection G.
- Round off the line at the shoulder.

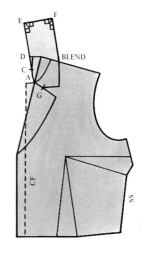

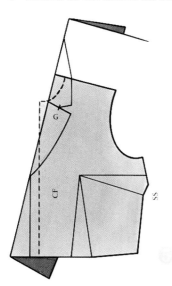

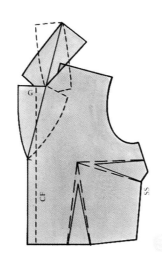

STEP 5

- Refold the paper on the roll line.
- Using the tracing wheel, trace the collar and the revers and mark at G.
- On the reverse side, trace the balance of the collar.
- Unfold the paper and pencil in the dotted lines.

STEP 6

- Retrace the collar, marking the centre back on the fold.
- Add 1 cm (⅜ in) seams all round and notch G, shoulder and centre back.
- Mark the grainline at the centre back.
- Cut two collars – one top collar, one under collar.

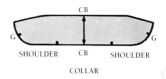

COLLAR

STEP 7

- Retrace the front.
- Add 1 cm (⅜ in) seams all round.
- Notch G, the breakpoint and the shoulder at the neck.
- Mark the grainline at the centre front.

STEP 8

- For the facing, trace the finished front (i.e. seams included), allowing about 6 to 7 cm (2⅜ to 2¾ in) width at the shoulder and the hem.
- Join from the shoulder to the hem as illustrated. This line may be straight, but is usually curved.

Necklines

SHAWL COLLAR

This collar may be attached to the front bodice or cut separately, depending on the quantity of fabric you have available and the desired effect of the collar. The shape of the shawl may be rounded, pointed or even notched.

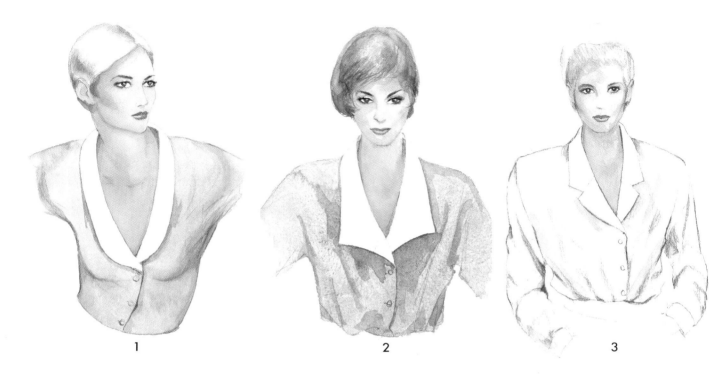

1   2   3

STEP 1

- Add 1.5 cm (⅝ in) to centre front to allow for overlap of the buttonstand.
- Establish the depth of the neckline.
- Mark this breakpoint A.
- Measure ½ of the back neck.
- Draw a roll line from A through B at the shoulder to C, so that BC equals ½ of the back neck.
- Establish the centre back width of the collar and square this line from C to D.
- Square the line from D down to E and then to A.

> ### HANDY HINT
>
> THIS CONSTRUCTION IS SIMPLER THAN THAT OF THE NOTCHED COLLAR. BY NOTCHING THE SHAWL COLLAR, A SIMILAR LOOK CAN BE ACHIEVED WITH FEWER COMPLICATIONS.

STEP 2

- Reshape AED according to the desired shape of the shawl as illustrated below.
- This shape allows for about a 2.5 cm (1 in) collarstand at the back.
- Add 1 cm (⅜ in) seams all round.

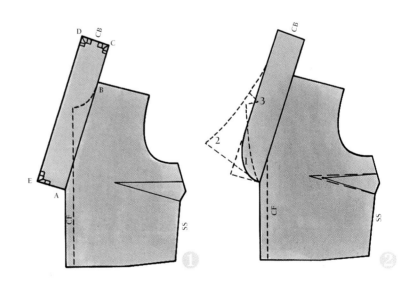

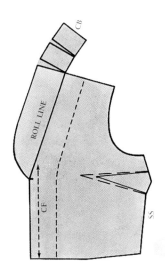

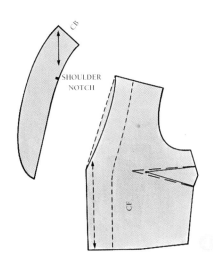

STEP 3

- For less collarstand and therefore
  a flatter fitting collar, slash the collar
  from the outer edge to the shoulder
  and also halfway between the shoulder
  and centre back.
- Spread slightly, thus curving the collar,
  as illustrated.

STEP 4

- For a separate collar, cut along the
  roll line.
- Curve the neckline slightly as illustrated.
- Add 1 cm (³⁄₈ in) seams all round.
- Notch the shoulder.
- Cut the collar with the CB seam
  on the bias.
- Cut four collars – two top collars,
  two under collars.

STEP 5

- Mark the facings about 6 to 7 cm
  (2³⁄₈ to 2³⁄₄ in) wide at the shoulder
  and at the hem.
- Join with the curved line as illustrated,
  parallel to the centre front and the
  neckline.

SHAWL COLLARS ARE POPULAR ON BLOUSES AND JACKETS

Necklines

Chapter VI

Sleeves

Sleeves are grouped into three major categories: the set-in sleeve, the raglan and the sleeve cut in one with the bodice. They may be fitted or full and may be cut to any desired length. Because of the constant

movement of one's arms. sleeves need to be comfortable. showing no signs of strain. The sleeve cap should fit smoothly. There must be enough room for the elbow to bend and the sleeve should hang evenly. conforming to the

natural curve of the arm. The single elbow dart gives the elbow a pointed look and may be divided evenly into multiple darts to curve the sleeve gently at the elbow. Your choice of sleeve is important and will influence the total silhouette of your garment.

FLARED/GATHERED HEM

The same construction applies to the sleeve, whether you decide on a bell-shaped sleeve or require elastic at the wrist. If a cuff is added to the gathered sleeve, then the sleeve needs to be shortened by approximately half the width of the cuff.

STEP 1

- Trace the outline of the basic sleeve.
- Slash from the hem to the dart point and close the dart.

STEP 2

- Divide the sleeve into 6 equal parts and mark these sections A to F.
- Drop the hem between C and E by about 2.5 cm (1 in).
- Curve the hem as illustrated.

STEP 3

- Slash the panels from the hem up to the cap, ensuring that all the pieces remain attached.
- Spread the panels A to F evenly to the desired width.

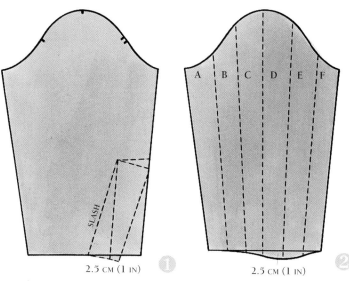

2.5 CM (1 IN)　　　2.5 CM (1 IN)

STEP 4

- Add 1 cm (⅜ in) seams.
- For the flared hem, either add a 1 cm (⅜ in) seam (to avoid puckering when stitching) or face this hem.
- For the elasticated hem, add 3 cm (about 1¼ in) to allow for a 1 cm (⅜ in) width elastic to be tunnelled through the hem. Notch the cap to correspond with the armholes.

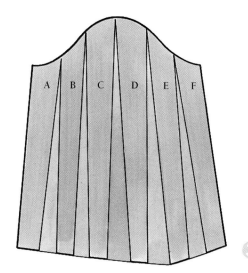

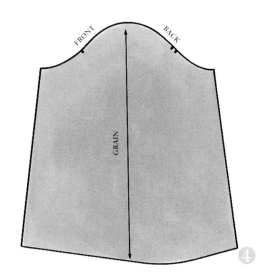

GATHERED/PLEATED CROWN

Puffed sleeves are very feminine and need to be cut in a suitable fabric to create the right effect. The more the crown is spread, the fuller the gathering or deeper the pleats will be. The more the crown is raised, the puffier the shape will be.

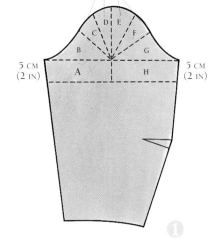

STEP 1

- Mark 5 dots 4 cm (about 1½ in) apart on the crown, placing the centre dot in the middle of the crown.
- Draw the lines as illustrated. Mark the sections A to H. Slash the crown from the top downwards and across to the sides. Sections C to F will be separated but, A, B, G and H must remain attached.
- Fold the sleeve in half to establish the grainline.

STEP 2

- Spread the sections evenly along the crown, thus raising A, H, B and G by about 2.5 cm (1 in) each.

STEP 3

- This crown may be gathered from B to G.
- Add 1 cm (⅜ in) seams all round, except for the hem, which should be 3 cm (1¼ in). Notch the front, the back and the shoulder as well as the points of gathering.

STEP 4

- For a pleated crown, carefully notch the gaps between B, C, D, E, F, and G to indicate the pleats, as illustrated.
- The centre pleat may be boxed or inverted if so desired, but the front and back pleats should face the direction indicated, in this way ensuring a pleasing fall or drape.

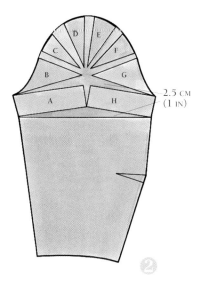

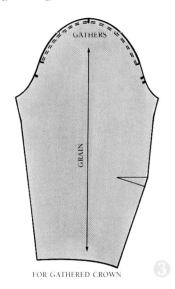

FOR GATHERED CROWN

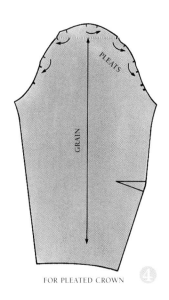

FOR PLEATED CROWN

Sleeves

SHIRT SLEEVE WITH CUFF

This sleeve may be pleated at the cuff or gathered, depending on the style of the garment. On average, the overarm neck to wrist measurement, including the cuff, is 1.5 cm (⅝ in) longer than the fitted sleeve without the cuff, thus measuring about 73 cm (28¾ in). This allows the sleeve to fall slightly over the cuff. Allowances must be made for the shoulder pads and certain style features.

STEP 1
- Trace the sleeve outline.
- Slash from the hem to the dart point and close the dart.

STEP 2
- Establish the cuff width.
- Shorten the sleeve by this measurement less 1.5 cm (⅝ in).
- Divide the sleeve into 4 equal parts and mark A to D. Drop the hem by 2.5 cm (1 in) between B and D.
- Curve the hem as illustrated.

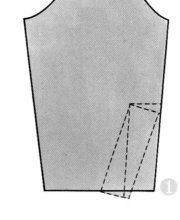

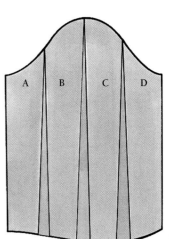

2.5 CM (1 IN)

STEP 3
- Slash the panels from the hem to the crown, ensuring all the pieces remain attached. Spread to the desired width.

STEP 4
- Mark E midway between the centre line and back seam.
- EF should measure about 8 cm (3¼ in).
- Mark F also midway between the centre line and back side seam.
- The cuff length should be about 23 cm (9 in).
- Mark the width on the fold, thus cutting two pieces for the shirt.
- If the cuff is shaped, 4 pieces need to be cut (i.e. top and under cuffs).
- Mark the pleats accordingly.
- Add 1 cm (⅜ in) seams all round the sleeve and the cuff, making the appropriate notches.
- Mark the grainlines as illustrated. The cuff will fit onto the sleeve from E, along the hem and back to E.

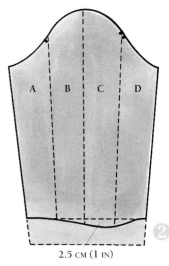

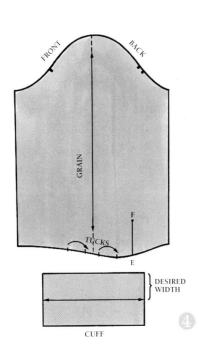

CUFF

DROPPED SHOULDER

This is the ideal sleeve for those who want to wear a sleeveless garment and yet do not want to expose their shoulders. Extending the shoulder seam in this way forms a slight cap sleeve. For a comfortable fit, it is necessary to drop the armhole slightly so that the new armhole measures closely to that of the regular armhole.

STEP 1

- Establish the shape of the neckline.
- Draw a line through the shoulder at the armhole, squared with the centre front, as illustrated.
- Extend the shoulder along this line by about 8 cm (about 3¼ in).
- Draw a line from this point to the new neckline.
- Drop the armhole by about 3 cm (1¼ in) and join to the shoulder.
- Repeat for the back bodice.

STEP 2

- To ensure that the armhole shape is correct, place the shoulders next to each other and, if necessary, curve slightly at the shoulder as indicated.
- Add 1 cm (⅜ in) seams all round.
- Notch the underarm and other appropriate places.
- This armhole may either be bound or faced to finish 5 cm (2 in) as illustrated by the dotted line.

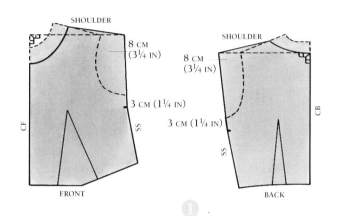

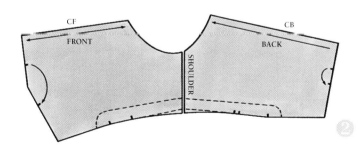

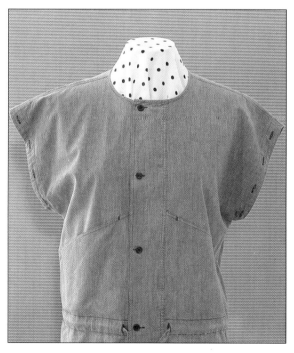

THIS EXTENDED SHOULDER FORMS A SLIGHT CAP SLEEVE

HANDY HINTS

ALL CORRESPONDING SEAMS SHOULD BE CHECKED ON EACH PATTERN PIECE TO ENSURE MATCHING SEAM LENGTHS AND TO ENABLE ONE TO ROUND OFF THE PERPENDICULAR SEAMS WHERE NECESSARY.

Sleeves

TWO-PIECE SLEEVE

The two-piece sleeve, also known as a tailored sleeve, is particularly used on jackets and some tailored dresses. When constructed correctly, it should hang in a curve that corresponds to the natural curve of the arm. The fit of this sleeve is also dependent on a well-fitting shoulder supported by a shoulder pad.

STEP 1

- Outline the sleeve.
- Slash from hem to dart point and close the dart.

STEP 2

- Establish the width of the sleeve at the hem and alter accordingly.
- Mark the centre line and fold in the side seams to meet at the centre line.
- Mark in the elbow line.
- Secure the centre line by using sticky tape.

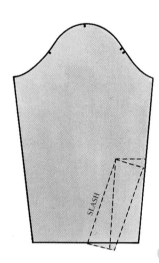

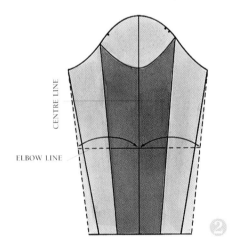

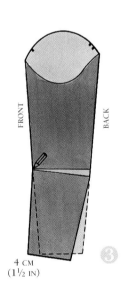

STEP 3

- Trace folded sleeve pattern, pivoting the sleeve at the front elbow line so that the hem moves forward by 4 cm (1½ in).
- Curve the elbow at the back.
- Mark in the top curve of the underarm

FRONT VIEW OF TWO-PIECE SLEEVE

4 CM (1½ IN)

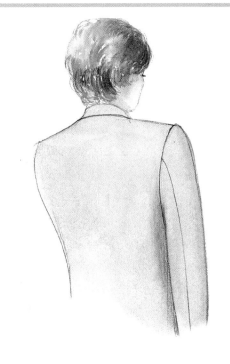

STEP 4

● Mark the sleeve seam lines within the sleeve
as illustrated, from 2.5 cm (1 in) at the top
to 2 cm (¾ in) at the elbow to 1.25 cm
(½ in) at the hem.

STEP 5

● Fold out the seams of the top sleeve as illustrated.
● If using the original folded pattern from Step 2,
slash along the lines in Step 4 to reveal the top
and the under sleeve.

STEP 6

● Add 1 cm (⅜ in) seams and a 3 cm (about
1¼ in) hem.
● Notch the front, centre and back on the crown.
● Notch the front elbow with one notch.
● Notch the back elbow with two notches on both
the top and under sleeves, as illustrated.
● Notch the centre of the underarm to correspond
with the side seam on the bodice.

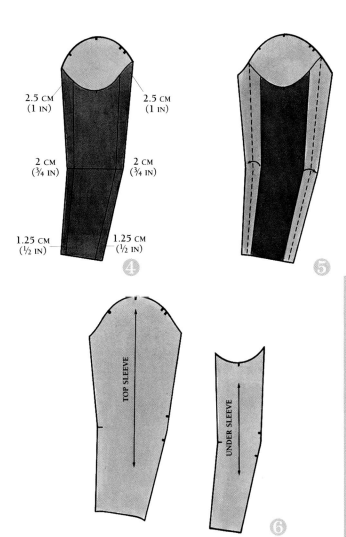

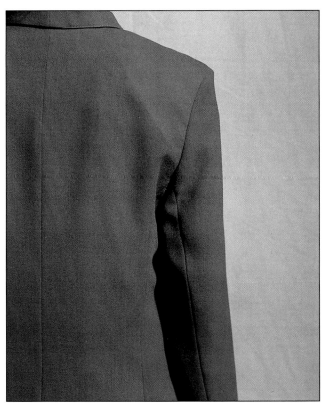

BACK VIEW OF A TWO-PIECE SLEEVE

Sleeves

RAGLAN SLEEVE

This sleeve is well liked for its comfortable fit and relatively easy construction. The shoulder curve becomes part of the sleeve shape created by a dart, a seam or even gathers and should conform to the shoulder and upper arm shape.

STEP 1

- On the front and back, drop the armhole by 2 cm (¾ in) and extend it by 1.5 cm (⅝ in) as illustrated.
- Likewise adjust sleeve to correspond with the front and back.

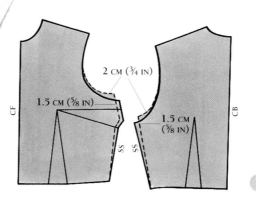

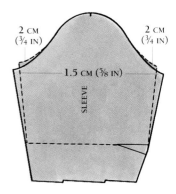

STEP 2

- On the front and the back, mark the raglan 2.5 cm (1 in) down from the shoulder on the neckline, 8 cm (about 3¼ in) diagonally from the shoulder at the armhole and 8 cm (about 3¼ in) from the side seam along the armhole, as illustrated.
- Curve this line slightly.
- Draw the curved lines on either side of the sleeve crown as illustrated. Mark A to G. (The depth of this curved line is immaterial).

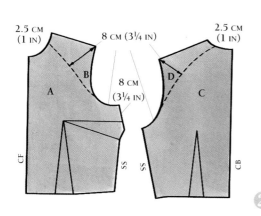

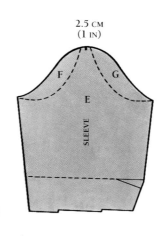

THIS RAGLAN FORMS A SHOULDER YOKE

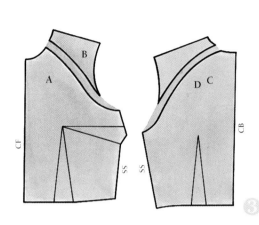

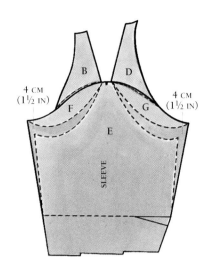

STEP 3

- Cut through the raglan lines on the front and back thus separating AB and CD.
- Slash the curved lines on the sleeve from the side seam to the crown so that the pieces still remain attached.
- Spread 4 cm (about 1½ in) at the underarm.
- Place the raglan section B alongside F and section D alongside G as illustrated.

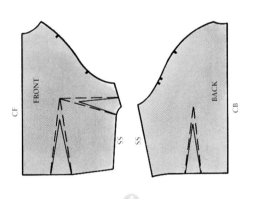

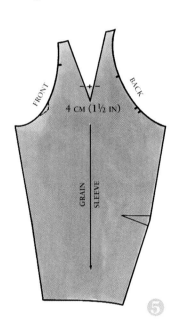

STEP 4

- Round off the raglan lines on the sleeve.
- Extend the shoulder dart on the sleeve by about 4 cm (about 1½ in).
- Add the seams all round. Make single corresponding notches on the front raglan and the front sleeve, and likewise double notches on the backs.

STEP 5 (OPTIONAL)

- For a two-piece sleeve, split the sleeve from the dart point on the shoulder through the centre of the sleeve at the elbow to the centre of the hem.
- Close the elbow dart on the back.
- Add the seams and notch accordingly.

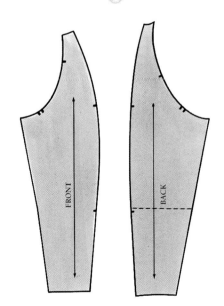

Sleeves

KIMONO/BATWING

The silhouettes of garments with these sleeves are almost T-shaped, creating soft folds when the arms are in a relaxed position. These sleeves are frequently used in the construction of T-shirts and sweatshirts.

STEP 1

● Outline the front and back bodices so that the shoulders touch at the neck, but are about 2.5 cm (1 in) apart at the armhole. This gives allowance for a shoulder pad, if so desired. If not, allow the shoulders to meet completely.
● Outline the sleeve so that the front sleeve crown overlaps the front armhole at the shoulder by 1.5 cm (⅝ in), ensuring that the sleeve is evenly placed at the underarm, as illustrated.

STEP 2

● Establish the sleeve seam position, usually about 4 cm (about 1½ in) down from the existing armhole.
● From this point on the sleeve, draw a curved line to meet the front and the back bodices at the side seam, as illustrated. Mark a new shoulder seam from the neck to the centre of the new dropped sleeve crown.

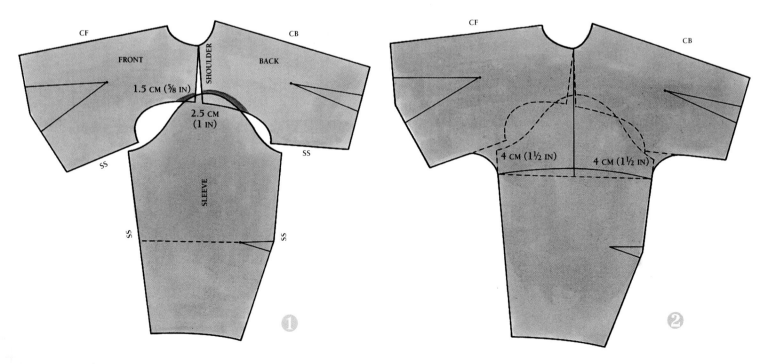

STEP 3

- Separate the front and back bodices and the sleeve.
- Add 1 cm ($^3/_8$ in) seams all round and a 3 cm ($1^1/_4$ in) hem. Eliminate the dart points and tuck the waistline instead, as illustrated, depending on your design.
- Notch the corresponding edges.
- Mark the grainlines parallel to the centre front and centre back seams and mark the grainline in the centre of the sleeve, perpendicular to the hem.

STEP 4

- For the short sleeve style, use the front and back bodices but eliminate the sleeve.
- The armhole may be faced or bound.
- The facing should finish off at 5 cm (2 in) in width.
- This construction may be used as an alternative to the dropped shoulder, because it has a similar cap effect.

STEP 5

- For the batwing style, follow Step 1 and then mark the new shoulder line from the neck through the centre of the elbow line to the centre of the hem line.
- Curve the line gently from the elbow to the front and back waist.
- This curved line should be gentle and not as acute as for the kimono.
- Split the sleeves and close the sleeve dart.
- Add the seams and mark overarm seams with corresponding notches.

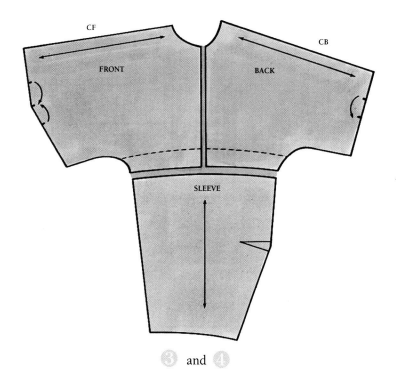

③ and ④

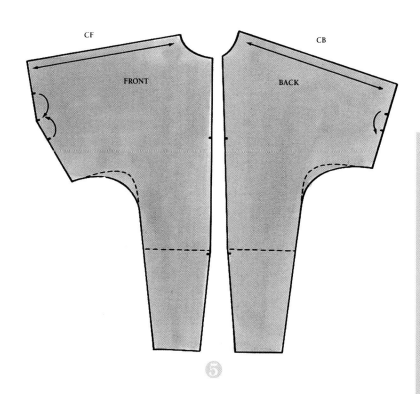

⑤

H A N D Y   H I N T S

THE BATWING SLEEVE IS NOT SEPARATE, BUT CUT IN ONE WITH THE BACK AND THE FRONT BODICES. THE UNDERARM SEAM MAY BE A CONTINUATION OF THE WAISTLINE IF MORE FULLNESS IS REQUIRED. HOWEVER, REMEMBER TO NOTCH THE SIDE SEAM IF ATTACHING TO A SKIRT.

Sleeves

B l o u s e s   a n d   T o p s

Prior to the 1480s the shirt was rarely seen and was always worn as an undergarment. At the time of Richard III. the shirt. worn by men. became an outer garment. It was fastened with bows and gathered at the neck and the cuffs. During the Renaissance. frills were added. By the 19th century. cravats and neckties trimmed the shirts. It was only during the Victorian period that women started wearing blouses with high necks and back fastenings. Blouses and shirts became evident in the early 1900s. In this chapter. various buttonstands with basic button positioning are explained. Pocket details may be found in the following chapter on jackets.

BUTTONSTANDS

A buttonstand may either be separate (to allow for bias grainlines in checked or striped fabric) or made with a separate facing, depending on the style or the width of the fabric used.

THE SEPARATE BUTTONSTAND

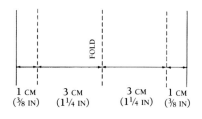
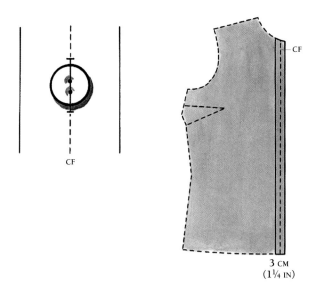

- On a separate buttonstand, buttonholes are made vertically in the centre of the buttonstand.
- The width of the buttonstand usually depends on the size of the button used, ensuring about a 1 cm ($^3/_8$ in) space from the edge of the button to the edge of the buttonstand.
- The average shirt or blouse buttons measure 1.25 cm ($^1/_2$ in) in width, thus making the buttonstand 3 cm (about $1^1/_4$ in) to 3.5 cm (about $1^3/_8$ in) wide, as illustrated.
- To mark a 3 cm (about $1^1/_4$ in) wide buttonstand, draw the lines parallel to the centre front, 1.5 cm ($^5/_8$ in) away on either side, remembering to add a 1 cm ($^3/_8$ in) seam for attaching the buttonstand.
  Cut the buttonstand on the fold, adding 1 cm ($^3/_8$ in) seams on either side, as illustrated.

THE ADD-ON BUTTONSTAND

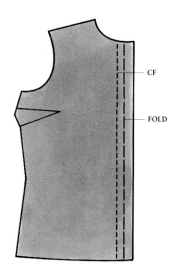

- On this type of buttonstand, button-holes may be vertical or horizontal, as desired.
- If vertical, apply the same ruling as for the separate stand.
- For the horizontal buttonhole, more width must be added to the button-stand so that from the edge of the buttonhole there is at least a 7 mm (about $^1/_4$ in) space to the edge of the buttonstand.
- The buttonhole must start 3 mm ($^1/_8$ in) beyond the centre front (CF) and made to the desired size.
- To add the buttonstand on to the shirt or blouse, mark the fold line about 1.5 cm ($^5/_8$ in) beyond the centre front line, then mark the edge at least 4 cm ($1^1/_2$ in) beyond the fold line, according to the width required.

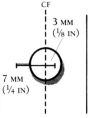

H A N D Y   H I N T
THERE IS NO NEED FOR A BACK NECK FACING WHEN MAKING A COLLAR, AS THE BACK NECK IS FINISHED OFF BY THE USE OF A COLLAR.

THE SEPARATE FACING

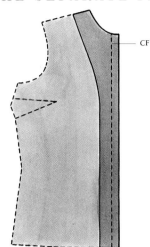

— CF

- This facing is used mainly on blouses where one wants to have no stitching or buttonstand visible, but one still, however, needs to use buttons and buttonholes to fasten the blouse. It is mostly used for open-necked shirts.
- Add 1.5 cm (⅝ in) to the centre front of the blouse.
- Make the facing about 5 cm (2 in) wide, parallel to the centre front and 5 cm (2 in) wide at the shoulder. Curve gently at about the bust level. Add 1 cm (⅜ in) seams to the shoulder, neck and the centre front. Add a 1 cm (⅜ in) seam all round to the blouse. The buttonholes may be vertical or horizontal, as desired.

BUTTON POSITIONING

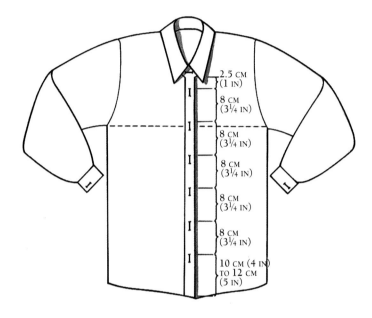

2.5 CM (1 IN)

8 CM (3¼ IN)

8 CM (3¼ IN)

8 CM (3¼ IN)

8 CM (3¼ IN)

8 CM (3¼ IN)

10 CM (4 IN) TO 12 CM (5 IN)

- When positioning buttons, please ensure that a button is placed on the bustline to ensure that the garment concerned does not gape.
- The distance between the buttons should be about 8 cm (about 3¼ in), depending on the style and size of the button.
- The first buttonhole on the buttonstand should be placed 2.5 cm (1 in) down from the neck seam as illustrated above right. This ensures a tidy fit at the collar. Please note that the buttonholes on the collarstand as well as those on the cuffs are made across. The illustration on the right shows the button positioning on a shirt or a blouse.

VARIOUS CUFF DETAILS

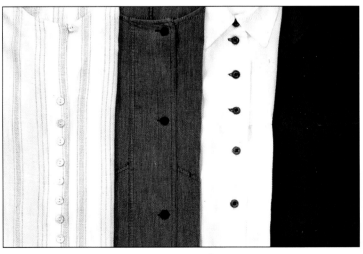

A VARIETY OF BUTTONSTANDS

COMBINING DETAILS

These styles may be created by using the basic darted blouse pattern or the dartless shirt pattern and combining the various details discussed in the previous chapters. Blouses tend to have softer, more feminine gathers or tucks, whereas shirts are more tailored and masculine in style.

PATTERN
- The basic darted blouse pattern.

FRONTS
- See page 36 for the yoke detail and refer to page 72 for the buttonstand. Straighten the side seams.

BACK
- Use the basic blouse back with the straightened side seams.

SLEEVE
- Combine page 61 and page 62.

COLLAR
- For the one-piece collar, see page 52.

SEAMS
- Add 1 cm (³⁄₈ in) seams all round.

PATTERN
- The basic dartless shirt pattern.

FRONTS
- Use the basic pattern on page 25 and refer to page 72 for the separate buttonstand.

POCKETS
- See page 81.

SLEEVE
- See page 62.

COLLAR
- See page 53 for a two-piece shirt collar.

SEAMS
- Add 1 cm (³⁄₈ in) seams all round.

PATTERN
- Use the basic darted blouse pattern.

FRONTS
- See page 37 for the yoke detail and refer to page 72 for the separate buttonstand. Straighten the side seams.

BACK
- Use the basic blouse back with straightened side seams, or repeat the front yoke detail at the back.

SLEEVE
- Combine page 61 and page 62.

COLLAR
- See the Peter Pan collar on page 51.

SEAMS
- Add 1 cm (³⁄₈ in) seams all round.

PATTERN
- Use the basic darted blouse pattern.

FRONTS
- See page 32 for the tuck detail and refer to page 72 for the buttonstand. Straighten the side seams.

BACK
- Use the basic blouse back with the straightened side seams.

SLEEVE
- See page 62.

COLLARS
- See page 45 for the tie neck.

SEAMS
- Add 1 cm (³⁄₈ in) seams all round.

HANDY HINT

FOR A MORE GENEROUS FIT TO THESE STYLES, ADD THE DESIRED AMOUNT TO THE SIDE SEAMS OF BOTH THE BACK AND THE FRONT, REMEMBERING TO INCREASE THE SLEEVE BY THE SAME AMOUNT.

Blouses and Tops

BASIC TOPS

The dartless hip foundation may be used to construct these patterns. It might be easier, however, to use the measurements from an existing garment to achieve the desired fit.

THE VEST
STEP 1

- Trace the outline of the dartless front and back.
- Drop the front neck by about 13 cm (about 5¼ in). Mark the shoulder strap centrally on the shoulder about 5 cm (2 in) wide.
- Reduce the neck by 1 cm (⅜ in) at the centre front.
- Reduce the armhole by about 1 cm (⅜ in) or as desired.
- Raise the armhole by 2 cm (¾ in).
- Mark the new neck and the armhole.
- Alter the back armhole as for the front.
- Mark the shoulder strap centrally and 5 cm (2 in) in width.
- Drop the back neck by 10 cm (4 in).
- Mark the new back neck and armhole.

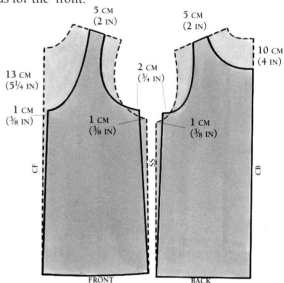

HANDY HINT

USE KNITTED FABRIC FOR THIS STYLE. FOR WOVENS, BUST DARTS ARE REQUIRED AND POSSIBLY A FRONT OPENING AS WELL.

STEP 2

- Cut the centre front and the centre back on the fold.
- Add a 1 cm (⅜ in) hem.
- Bind the armhole and the neck (no seams needed when binding). Wovens may be faced.

THE T-SHIRT

- Establish the centre back length and the desired width of the T-shirt. Use the dartless hip foundation pattern and alter the length and width accordingly.
- Follow the instructions for the kimono sleeve on page 68.
- Part the shoulder seams as for the shoulder pad. This also allows for a looser fit at the armhole.
- Establish the length and hem circumference of the sleeve and alter accordingly.
- Remove 2.5 cm (1 in) to 3 cm (about 1¼ in) from the back and front neck to accommodate the ribbing.
- Add 1 cm (⅜ in) seams all round, as well as to the hem.
- Cut the ribbing width on the fold with 1 cm (⅜ in) seams and length according to the elasticity of the ribbing used.

THE SWEATSHIRT

- Use the dartless hip foundation pattern.
- Establish the centre back length and width of the sweatshirt and alter the pattern accordingly. Follow the kimono sleeve instructions on page 68.
- Part the shoulder seams as for the shoulder pad.
- Close the sleeve dart, thus straightening the seam and increasing the width at the hem.
- Shorten the sleeve by 3.5 cm (1⅜ in) to accommodate the 5 cm (2 in) width ribbed cuff. A 1.5 cm (⅝ in) ease has been included to allow for the overhang or blousing of the sleeve at the cuff.
- Remove 3 cm (about 1¼ in) from the front and back neck to accommodate the neck ribbing.
- Allow for a 5 cm (2 in) width ribbing on the front and the back at the hem.
- Cut all the ribbing width on the fold. The length will depend on the elasticity of the ribbing used.
- Add 1 cm (⅜ in) seams to all the pieces.

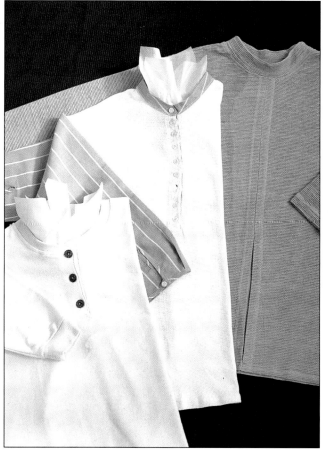

WOVENS AND KNITS MAY BE USED FOR SWEATSHIRTS

HANDY HINTS

MAKE SURE THAT YOUR HEAD CAN FIT THROUGH THE NECK OF THE T-SHIRT AS WELL AS THE SWEATSHIRT. WHEN USING WOVENS, THE MINIMUM NECK MEASUREMENT MUST BE AT LEAST THAT OF THE HEAD CIRCUMFERENCE. IF NOT, A SHORT ZIP OR A HALF BUTTONSTAND SHOULD BE ADDED.

Blouses and Tops

CHAPTER VIII

Jackets

The fit of all jackets varies considerably depending on the shape or silhouette that is desired. The length may range from the waistline to as far down as the knee. The basic jacket pattern is fairly snug-fitting and more ease may be added to the width for a looser fit. Once again, new styles can be created by integrating various ideas from within this book. Once you realize that there are no short cuts to a professional finish.

the tailored jacket is not as difficult as it first seems. The jacket should be interlined correctly to avoid sagging or wrinkling without making it stiff and uncomfortable. Make sure that the lining does not pull or interfere with the fall of the jacket.

LININGS

Linings are usually cut the same width as the pattern but adding a centre back tuck allows for more comfort and ease. The sleeve lengths are cut shorter to prevent the lining from showing.

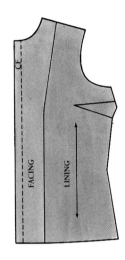

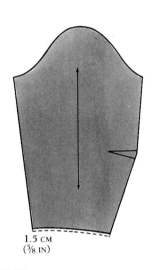

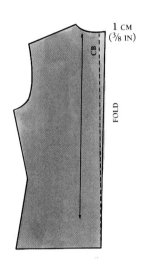

FRONT
- Trace the jacket front.
- Mark facing to desired width.
- The balance of the front will become the lining.
- Add 1 cm (3⁄8 in) seams all round including the hem.

SLEEVE
- Outline the jacket sleeve and shorten by 1.5 cm (5⁄8 in).
- Add 1 cm (3⁄8 in) all round including the hem.

BACK
- Trace the jacket back. For the centre back tuck, add 1 cm (3⁄8 in) from the neck to nothing at the hem. Cut CB on the fold. Add 1 cm (3⁄8 in) seams all round including the hem.

FACINGS FOR UNLINED JACKETS

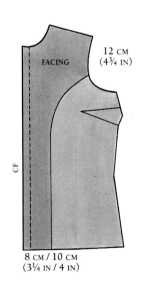

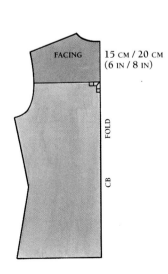

FRONT
- Trace the jacket front. Mark the facing 8 cm to 10 cm (about 3¼ in to 4 in) wide at the hem. Curve gently to the armhole about 12 cm (4¾ in) down from the shoulder – this will give more body to the shoulder area. Add 1 cm (3⁄8 in) seams to the CF, the neck, the shoulder and the armhole.

BACK
- The back facing is optional, but preferable. It also gives more body to the back shoulder and neatens the jacket.
- Trace the jacket back and mark the facing 15 cm to 20 cm (about 6 in to 8 in) down from the neck at the centre back.
- Square this line.
- Cut CB on the fold. Add 1 cm (3⁄8 in) seams to the neck, the shoulder and the armhole.

POCKETS

Shirt pockets may vary between 8 cm (about 3¼ in) and 14 cm (5½ in) in width and 8 cm (about 3¼ in) and 16 cm (6¼ in) in length. This will depend on the style chosen. The pocket position is generally about 20 cm to 25 cm (about 8 in to 10 in) below the centre of the shoulder, and perpendicular to the centre front. Jacket pockets may vary between 12 cm (4¾ in) and 16 cm (6¼ in) in width and about 23 cm (9 in) in depth. Separate pocket flaps should be cut slightly wider than the pockets to ensure that the pockets are covered on either side. They are usually attached 1 cm (⅜ in) above the pockets. Remember to mark these positions carefully. The hem or facing of the pocket should not be less than 2.5 cm (1 in) in width; the seams may be 1 cm (⅜ in).

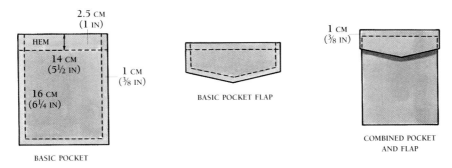

BASIC POCKET

BASIC POCKET FLAP

COMBINED POCKET AND FLAP

For a pleated pocket, split the basic pocket in half vertically and spread accordingly.

 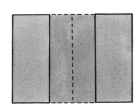 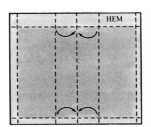 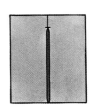

STEP 1
● Slash through the central line.

STEP 2
● Spread according to the pleat required. Here an inverted pleat is illustrated.

STEP 3
● Add 1 cm (⅜ in) seams all round, except the hem, which should be 2.5 cm (1 in).

HERE ARE SOME SIMPLE BUT EFFECTIVE POCKET VARIETIES

Jackets

COMBINING DETAILS

Various jacket patterns can be made by using the basic jacket pattern and combining the different details discussed in the previous chapters. Here are some examples.

JACKET WITH SHAWL COLLAR

BACK AND FRONT
- Use the basic jacket pattern with darts. Establish the centre back length. Follow the instructions for Style B on page 100. Panel the front accordingly. Curve to the hem at the centre front.

COLLAR
- See the shawl collar on page 56 using Steps 1 to 3.

SLEEVE
- See the two-piece sleeve on page 64.

POCKET
- Opening 15 cm (6 in). Depth as desired. Attach the inside seam with corresponding shape. Curve the other bottom corner.

FACINGS AND LINING
- Use the centre front panels for facings. Refer to page 80 for linings.

SEAMS
- Add 1 cm (³⁄₈ in) to all the pattern pieces; 3 cm (about 1¼ in) for the jacket hem, 2.5 cm (1 in) for the sleeve hem, and 3 cm (about 1¼ in) for the pocket hem. Make the appropriate notches.

BOXY DOUBLE-BREASTED BLAZER

BACK AND FRONT
- Use the basic dartless jacket pattern on page 23. Establish the centre back length. The centre back seam is optional. Use the double-breasted front.

COLLAR, SLEEVE AND POCKET
- For the collar, follow the instructions for the notched collar on page 54, drawing a roll line from the break-point on the double-breasted front to the extended shoulder at the neck. Continue as for the single-breasted, Steps 1 to 7.
- For the sleeve, see the two-piece sleeve on page 64.
- For the pocket, make the opening 15 cm (6 in). Depth as desired (about 20 cm or 8 in). The pocket may be attached in the side seam.

FACINGS AND LINING
- Trace the front, draw a parallel line from hem to break point about 16 cm (6¼ in) wide, then continue to mid-shoulder. Curve the line gently. Refer to page 80 for linings.

SEAMS
- Add 1 cm (³⁄₈ in) to all the pattern pieces; 3 cm (about 1¼ in) for the jacket hem, 2.5 cm (1 in) for the sleeve hem, and 3 cm (about 1¼ in) for the pocket hem. Make appropriate notches.

FLARED CAR COAT

A car coat is a long A-line jacket with
a generous flared hem.

PATTERN
- Use the basic dartless single-breasted jacket.

BACK
- Establish the centre back length. Slash from the
  hem upwards and spread to the desired width.

FRONT
- Slash and spread the front to correspond with
  the back. Add on buttonstand as on page 72.

COLLAR
- See the one-piece shirt collar on page 52.
  Make slightly wider; round off the points.

SLEEVE
- Follow instructions for raglan sleeve on page 66.

FACING
- Front width about 8 cm (about 3¼ in) curving gently
  to the raglan seam and maintaining the same width.

LINING
- Optional. Refer to page 80 for linings.

SEAMS
- Add 1 cm (⅜ in) to all the pieces. Hem 3 cm (1¼ in);
  sleeve hem 2.5 cm (1 in).

BOMBER JACKET

The length varies from the waist to the hip.
The band may be fitted or elasticated.

BACK AND FRONT
- Use basic dartless jacket. Establish centre back length.
  Tuck hem to fit band. Make front to correspond with
  back, tucking hem to fit band.

BAND
- Establish the width of the band. Cut double the
  width. Length to fit snugly on the hip.

COLLAR
- Refer to the one-piece shirt collar on page 52.

SLEEVE
- See the shirt sleeve with cuff on page 62.

POCKET
- See the pleated pocket with the flap on page 81.
  Opening 14 cm (5½ in).

FACINGS AND LINING
- Facings' width about 6 cm (2½ in) from band curving
  gently to shoulder. Linings optional. Sleeve and body
  length same as jacket, as lining will be attached to cuff
  and band respectively. Refer to page 80 for linings.

SEAMS
- 1 cm (⅜ in) all round except CF seams to be 1.5 cm
  (⅝ in) for the open end zip.

Jackets

CHAPTER IX

Skirts

Skirt lengths and shapes change seasonally, but the basic methods of construction remain the same. They play a major role in classifying a silhouette. The degree of width at the hemline and the

waistline may vary, classifying the skirts as either slim, full or shaped. Slim skirts may have soft fullness at the waist and not at the hemline, or may be developed with flat pressed pleats or straight panels, still retaining a slim look. Full and shaped skirts achieve their width at the hemline and sometimes also at the waistline by using panels, gathers, pressed or unpressed pleats and circles. Variations to the divided skirts, more widely known as culottes, may be achieved by following the same principles given for skirts.

WAISTBAND

The waistband measurement must correspond to that of the skirt or trouser waist, and then a 2.5 cm (1 in) underlap must be added for the button. The width will vary according to the style.

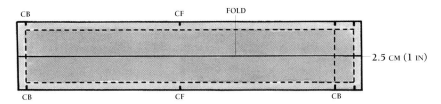

Add 1 cm (³⁄₈ in) seams all round and notch the fold line, the centre front, both the centre backs and the extension seam as illustrated. This waistband construction will apply to all skirts and trousers.

THE ELASTIC MEASUREMENT GUIDE

These guides might vary slightly according to the width and finish of the elastic. They will apply to both the skirts and the trousers.

THE FULLY ELASTICATED WAIST

SIZES	UK US 32 10 8	UK US 34 12 10	UK US 36 14 12	UK US 38 16 14	UK US 40 18 16	UK US 42 20 18
Finished measurement	55 cm	60 cm	65 cm	70 cm	75 cm	80 cm
IMPERIAL MEASUREMENTS	22 in	24 in	26 in	28 in	30 in	32 in
Minimum stretch measurement	89 cm	94 cm	99 cm	104 cm	109 cm	114 cm
IMPERIAL MEASUREMENTS	35 in	37 in	39 in	41 in	43 in	45 in

THE THREE-QUARTER ELASTICATED WAIST

Finished measurement	57 cm	62 cm	67 cm	72 cm	77 cm	82 cm
IMPERIAL MEASUREMENTS	23 in	25 in	27 in	29 in	31 in	33 in
Minimum stretch measurement	89 cm	94 cm	99 cm	104 cm	109 cm	114 cm
IMPERIAL MEASUREMENTS	35 in	37 in	39 in	41 in	43 in	45 in

THE HALF ELASTICATED WAIST

Finished measurement	59 cm	64 cm	69 cm	74 cm	79 cm	84 cm
IMPERIAL MEASUREMENTS	23¼ in	25¼ in	27¼ in	29¼ in	31¼ in	33¼ in
Minimum stretch measurement	89 cm	94 cm	99 cm	104 cm	109 cm	114 cm
IMPERIAL MEASUREMENTS	35 in	37 in	39 in	41 in	43 in	45 in

ZIPS

The normal zip length on a skirt is 20 cm (8 in). 18 cm (7 in) zips may be used on full skirts. Bear in mind that when open, the skirt must be able to slip over the bottom comfortably. Trouser zips are normally 18 cm (7 in) in length.

BASIC FOUR-PANELLED FLARED SKIRT

STEP 1

AB – Centre front length.

AC – 18 cm (7 in).

CD – ½ hip circumference plus a 2.5 cm (1 in) ease. Square this line.

CE – ⅓ of CD. Draw an arc above D about 25 cm (almost 10 in) long, pivoting at E.

BF – ¼ hem circumference. Square the line from B.

FG – Equals BF. First place the square touching point F for the lower edge and touching the outer curve of the arc for the centre back line, ensuring that BF = FG. Draw FG and GH.

GH – Equals AB plus 6 mm (¼ in).

STEP 2

BJ – Equals ½ BF.

GK – Equals ½ FG.

JK – Connect and then slightly curve the line.

AL – ¼ AH.
Square the line from A.

HM – Equals AL.
Square the line from H.

LM – Connect and then slightly curve the line.

LN – Equals ½ LM.

JO – Equals ½ JK.

NO – Connect for the side seam.

STEP 3

OP – Equals BC which equals GQ.
Draw a curved hip line from C through P to Q.

NR – Equals the reduction at the waistline to correspond with your waist measurement and should be about 1.25 cm (½ in).

RP – Connect. Crossmark the side seam.

STEP 4

● Split the side seam.

● Add 1 cm (⅜ in) seams all round except for the centre back which is to have a 1.5 cm (⅝ in) seam for the zip.

● The hem should be about 1 cm (⅜ in) or narrower to prevent a roping effect when stitching. Make the appropriate notches.

● Mark the grainline parallel to the side seam.

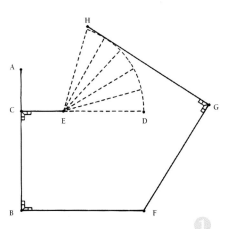

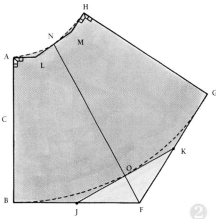

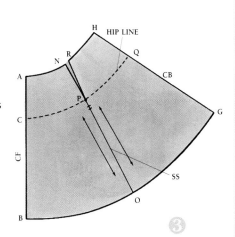

Skirts

SIX-GORED SKIRT

This skirt has six panels or gores and a hem circumference of about 152 cm (60 in). This measurement may also be altered as desired. The opening or the zip needs to be on the left-hand side seam so that the centre front and centre back panels can be cut on the fold. This skirt is very flattering because of its slimming effect. You may also use this method to make an eight-gored skirt.

STEP 1

- Follow Step 1 and Step 2 of the instructions for a 4-panelled skirt on the previous page; using all the same measurements except for the hem circumference, which should be 152 cm (60 in).

STEP 2

- Mark the hip line so that BC = OP = GQ.
- Mark the side front panel 10 cm (4 in) from the centre front at the hip and 14 cm (5½ in) from the centre front at the hem. Join these points and extend to the waistline.
- Mark the side back panel also 10 cm (4 in) from the centre back at the hip and 14 cm (5½ in) from the centre back at the hem. Join these points and extend to the waistline.

STEP 3

- Reduce the waist on the side panels by about 6 mm (¼ in) on the side front, 4 cm (about 1½ in) on each side of the side seam and 1.2 cm (½ in) on the side back, as illustrated.
- Ensure that the finished waist corresponds to the required waist measurement, and alter accordingly.
- Crossmark the seams.
- Split up the panels by adding 1 cm (⅜ in) seams all round, except on the left side seams which should be 1.5 cm (⅝ in) to accommodate a zip.
- The hem may be 1 cm to 3 cm (⅜ in to about 1¼ in) as desired.
- Mark the centre front and the centre back on the fold.
- The grainlines for the side panels should be marked in the centre of each panel.

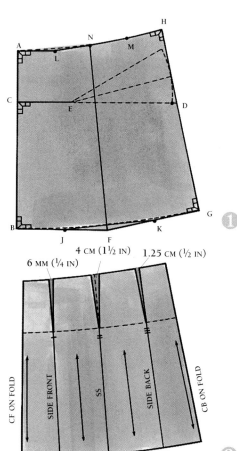

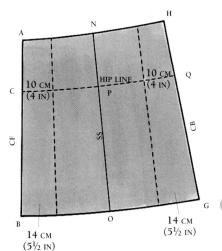

SIX-GORED SKIRT WITH INVERTED PLEATS

Steps may be added on to gores for pleats as shown here.

- Follow the instructions on the previous page for the 6-gored skirt.
- Establish the length and depth of the pleat and add on to the side front as illustrated.
- Make the pleat facing double the depth of the pleat.

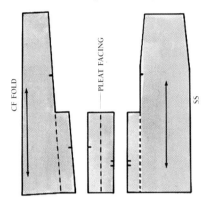

- Add 1 cm (³⁄₈ in) seams to all the edges except the hem which should be 3 cm (about 1¼ in) and the left side seam which should be 1.5 cm (⁵⁄₈ in) to allow for a zip.
- Notch appropriately.
- This pleat may be repeated at the side back seam, as desired.

CENTRE BACK VENT (PLEAT WITH A SLIT)

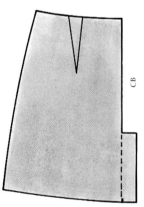

LEFT BACK

Adding a centre back vent to a skirt allows the same freedom as that of a slit, and yet does not expose the leg in the same way. This detail is also used on jackets.

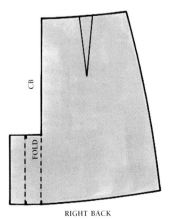

RIGHT BACK

- Establish the length of the centre back vent. The depth of the vent should be about 3 cm to 5 cm (about 1¼ in to 2 in) as desired. Add this on to the centre back on the left back as illustrated.
- On the right back, add double the depth added on to the left back, to allow for the fold back.
- Add a 1.5 cm (⁵⁄₈ in) seam to both the centre backs for the zip and 1 cm (³⁄₈ in) seams to all the other edges, except the hem which may range from 1 cm to 3 cm (³⁄₈ in to about 1¼ in), depending on the fabric used.
- Notch the centre back and the fold line of the vent.
- This slit may be stitched closed, forming a knife pleat.

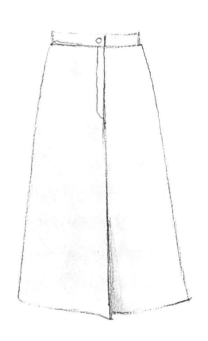

Skirts

DIRNDL SKIRT

A dirndl skirt is a skirt gathered onto a waistband. Take care when choosing your fabric as the effect can be so varied. Tucks may be replaced by gathers following the same instructions as for the sleeve cap on page 61.

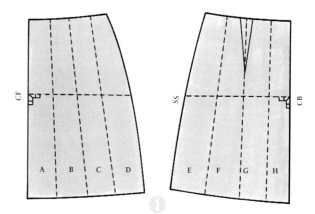

STEP 1

- See the beginning of the chapter for the waistband draft.
- Mark the front and back working lines perpendicular to CF and CB respectively.
- Divide the front and the back into four equal parts, marking A to H.

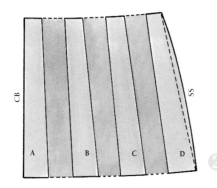

STEP 2

- Slash through the spreading lines on the front and the back.
- Draw the second working line.
- Spread the panels ABCD and EFGH according to the fullness required, matching the first and second working lines.

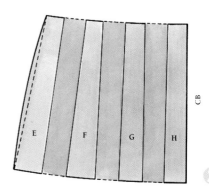

STEP 3

- Gently curve the waistline and the hem on the front and the back.
- Straighten the side seam, eliminating the curve at the hip.
- Cut the front on the fold or use a centre front seam, depending on the width of the fabric.
- Add 1 cm ($\frac{3}{8}$ in) seams all round, except for the centre back which requires a 1.5 cm ($\frac{5}{8}$ in) seam for the zip. The hem may be 1 cm to 3 cm ($\frac{3}{8}$ in to about $1\frac{1}{4}$ in).

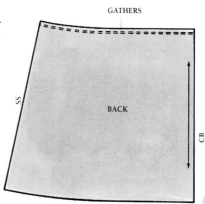

DIRNDL SKIRT WITH BASQUE

This skirt is more flattering than the basic dirndl because of the close fit around the hip. Basque is another term used for a hip yoke.

PLEATED

TUCKED

GATHERED

STEP 1

- Measure the lower hip, adding some ease.
- Make the width of the yoke 18 cm (about 7 in) plus 7 cm (about 3 in) for elasticizing the waist, using a 3 cm (about 1¼ in) elastic. The yoke width may vary from 15 cm to 20 cm (about 6 in to 8 in).
- Draw a rectangle 25 cm (i.e. 18 cm + 7 cm) x hip measurement OR 10 in (7 in + 3 in) x hip measurement.
- Add 1 cm (³⁄₈ in) seams and notch waist.

4 CM (1½ IN)

3 CM (1¼ IN)

YOKE (CUT 1)

18 CM (7 IN)

STEP 2

- Establish the length of the skirt and draw the rectangle according to the desired length by twice the hip measurement. This is the usual amount of fullness. For more fullness, up to 3 times the hip measurement may be added.
- Add 1 cm (³⁄₈ in) seams all round. The grainlines may depend on the width, stripe or type of fabric used.

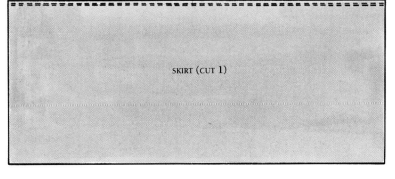

GATHERS OR TUCKS

SKIRT (CUT 1)

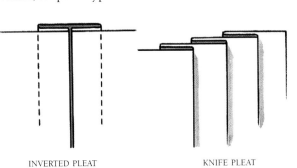

INVERTED PLEAT

KNIFE PLEAT

- Knits must always be cut with CF and CB on the grain, not across.
- This skirt may be tucked onto the basque, the depth of tucks as desired.
- For pleats, however, 3 times the hip measurement is needed for a full underlay, using either knife or inverted pleats. Tiers of frills may be joined together in this way to create a carnival or gypsy style.

CIRCULAR SKIRTS

Circular skirts may be cut with various amounts of fullness, i.e. full circle, ¾ circle or ½ circle. They may be cut in one piece or panelled, depending on the width of fabric used. There are formulas by which one can determine the approximate radius needed to mark the waistlines of any circular skirts.

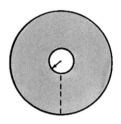

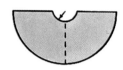

FULL CIRCLE

- Waist minus 4 cm (1½ in) divided by 6 = radius
  e.g. 70 cm (28 in) – 4 cm (1½ in) = 66 cm (26½ in) ÷ 6 = 11 cm (4½ in) radius

¾ CIRCLE

- Waist minus 4 cm (1½ in) divided by 4.5 = radius
  e.g. 70 cm (28 in) – 4 cm (1½ in) = 66 cm (26½ in) ÷ 4.5 = 14.6 cm (5⅞ in) radius

½ CIRCLE

- Waist minus 4 cm (1½ in) divided by 3 = radius
  e.g. 70 cm (28 in) – 4 cm (1½ in) = 66 cm (26½ in) ÷ 3 = 22 cm (8⅞ in) radius

FULL CIRCLE

- Fold the paper in half for a 2-piece skirt and in half again for a 1-piece skirt. Determine the radius by using the formula opposite and mark the waistline. Establish the skirt length and mark it equidistant from the waistline.

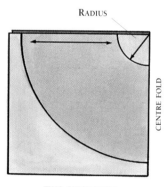

RADIUS

CENTRE FOLD

TWO-PIECE SKIRT

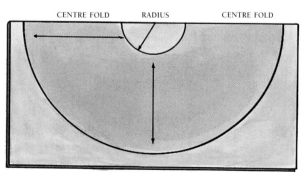

CENTRE FOLD   RADIUS   CENTRE FOLD

ONE-PIECE SKIRT

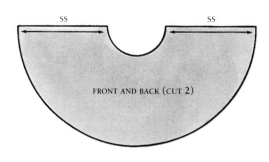

FRONT AND BACK (CUT 2)

- Add a 1 cm (³⁄₈ in) seam to the waist and one side of the 2-piece skirt and 1.5 cm (⁵⁄₈ in) to the other side of a 2-piece skirt for a zip. On a 1-piece skirt, add a 1 cm (³⁄₈ in) seam to the waist only. Make a 20 cm (8 in) slit at the centre back for the zip. The hem on both skirts should be as narrow as possible; about 6 mm (¹⁄₄ in). If the waist is to be gathered or elasticated, ensure that this has been allowed for, before determining its radius. In most cases the 2-piece skirt is used, as very few fabrics are wide enough to cut a full circle!

¹⁄₂ CIRCLE

STEP 1

- Fold paper in half. Determine radius using formula above. Mark waistline. Establish skirt length and mark equidistant from waistline.

STEP 2

- Add 1.5 cm (⁵⁄₈ in) seams to centre backs, 1 cm (³⁄₈ in) to waist and 6 mm (¹⁄₄ in) for hem.

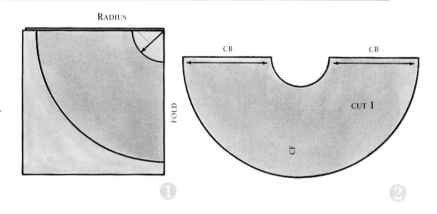

³⁄₄ CIRCLE

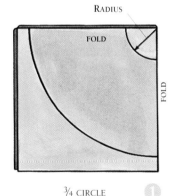

³⁄₄ CIRCLE

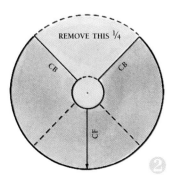

STEP 1

- Fold the paper into quarters as illustrated. Use the formula above to determine radius.
- Mark the waistline.
- Establish the skirt length and mark it equidistant from the waistline.

STEP 2

- Open out the paper and divide it into four quarters. Remove one quarter as illustrated. Fold the remaining three-quarters in half, matching the straight edges.

- This will determine the centre front. Add a 1.5 cm (⁵⁄₈ in) seam to both the CB edges, 1 cm (³⁄₈ in) to the waist and 6 mm (¹⁄₄ in) to the hem.

STEP 3

- For a 2-piece skirt, split the pattern on the fold line of a ³⁄₄ circle. Fold in half again to determine the grainline.
- Add 1.5 cm (⁵⁄₈ in) to the left side seams and 1 cm (³⁄₈ in) to the right side seams and waist. The hem should be 6 mm (¹⁄₄ in).

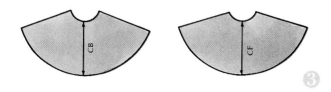

Skirts

93

THE CULOTTE

The culotte is a versatile and comfortable garment that can be worn by anyone, irrespective of shape or size. A selection of fabrics can also be used, depending on the look required. The basic culotte can easily be converted into a variety of styles following the instructions given for skirts.

FRONT

STEP 1

Trace the front skirt outline

AB – Equals centre front.

CD – Equals side seam.

AE – Equals crotch depth plus 2.5 cm (1 in).

CF – Equals AE.

STEP 2

EG – ½ EF minus 2.5 cm (1 in). Square this line.

BH – Equals EG. Square this line.

GH – Join.

STEP 3

EI – 5 cm (2 in). Draw a diagonal line from E to I.

GI – Equals IJ. Join G to I; I to J.

STEP 4

● Add 1 cm (³⁄₈ in) seams all round, except for the zip seam which should be 1.5 cm (⁵⁄₈ in), either at the CB or on the left-hand side. The hem may be 1 cm to 3 cm (³⁄₈ in to about 1¼ in), depending on the fabric used.

● Notch the seams.

● Mark the grain parallel to the centre front.

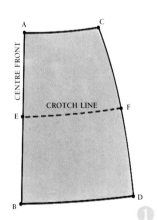

HANDY HINT

THE FRONT CROTCH IS ALWAYS SHORTER THAN THE BACK. ALTHOUGH 2.5 CM (1 IN) IS REMOVED FROM THE FRONT, IT IS ADDED AGAIN ON TO THE BACK CROTCH.

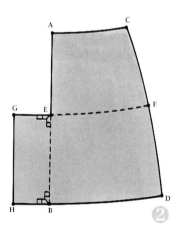

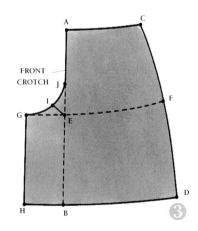

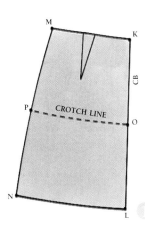

BACK

STEP 1

Trace the skirt back outline.

KL – Equals centre back.

MN – Equals side seam.

KO – Equals crotch depth plus 2.5 cm (1 in).

MP – Equals KO.

STEP 2

OQ – ½ OP plus 2.5 cm (1 in). Square this line.

LR – Equals OQ. Square this line.

QR – Join.

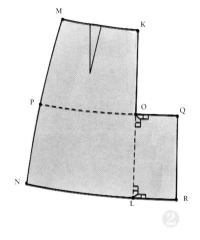

STEP 3

OS – 6.5 cm (2½ in).
Draw a diagonal
line from O
to S.

QS – Equals ST.
Join Q to S,
S to T.

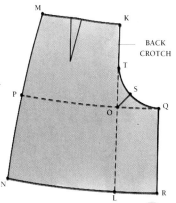

STEP 4

- Add 1 cm (⅜ in)
  seams all round, except for the zip seam which
  should be 1.5 cm (⅝ in), either at the CB or the
  left-hand side. The hem may be 1 cm to 3 cm
  (⅜ in to 1¼ in).
- Notch the seams.
- Mark the grainline parallel to the centre back.

WAISTBAND

Refer to the draft on page 86.

THIS CULOTTE HAS A TUCKED FRONT AS WELL AS AN ELASTICATED WAIST

HANDY HINT

CULOTTES MAY BE LENGTHENED TO CREATE PALAZZO PANTS.
IN DAYS GONE BY THE CULOTTE WAS ANOTHER NAME FOR
BREECHES. TODAY IT DESCRIBES FLARED KNEE-LENGTH
TROUSERS CUT TO LOOK LIKE A SKIRT. A GOLF-STYLED
CULOTTE CAN BE CREATED BY ADDING AN INVERTED PLEAT
TO THE CENTRE FRONT AND THE CENTRE BACK.

Skirts

C H A P T E R   X

D r e s s e s

Most women tend to wear separates for work and at home, rather than dresses, as they are easier to mix and match.

There are times when a dress is more appropriate than a blouse and a skirt. One-piece dresses can be very slimming, especially the princess line styles. However, some people might prefer a fitting bodice with a fuller skirt. In the

1920s the dropped waist was very popular. The shift was introduced in the 1960s, as well as the smock and the tent silhouettes. Whether the waistline is raised, lowered or even eliminated, the options are endless.

Dresses

97

FRONT BODICE

WAIST

2.5 CM
(1 IN)

2.5 CM
(1 IN)

CENTRE FRONT

SIDE FRONT

5 CM
(2 IN)

5 CM (2 IN)

EMPIRE LINE

In about 1800 the chemise dress altered. The bodice was cut just below the bust and the neckline squared. This style was popularized by the ladies of Napoleon's court and was named after the emperor himself. Since then, its appeal has waxed and waned.

STEP 1

- Trace the front and back of the hip length pattern.
- For the sleeveless armhole, reduce the armhole by 1 cm ($\frac{3}{8}$ in) and raise by 2 cm ($\frac{3}{4}$ in) on the front and back.
- Drop the front neck by about 13 cm (about $5\frac{1}{4}$ in) and reduce by 1 cm ($\frac{3}{8}$ in).
- Drop the back neck by about 5 cm (2 in).
- Mark shoulder 6 cm ($2\frac{3}{8}$ in) wide in the middle of shoulder.
- Join to the new necklines and armholes.
- Mark the empire line about $\frac{1}{3}$ up on the centre front, keeping the line parallel to the waist on the front and the back. For a closer fit, make the front dart 6 mm ($\frac{1}{4}$ in) deeper on either side at the empire line.

STEP 2

- Cut out the front bodice along the empire line and the panels along the dart lines.
- Cut out the vertical dart on the bodice, slash the side dart and close, thereby enlarging the vertical dart.
- Cut out the back bodice along the empire line and the panels along the dart lines.
- Extend the skirt panels to the desired length, and mark the slash lines 2.5 cm (1 in) from the waist and 5 cm (2 in) from the hem on all the panels as illustrated.

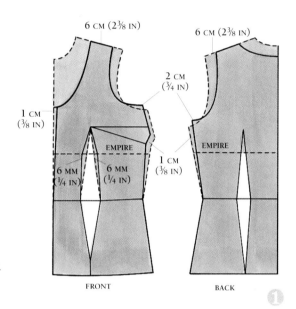

6 CM ($2\frac{3}{8}$ IN)

6 CM ($2\frac{3}{8}$ IN)

2 CM
($\frac{3}{4}$ IN)

1 CM
($\frac{3}{8}$ IN)

EMPIRE

EMPIRE

1 CM
($\frac{3}{8}$ IN)

6 MM
($\frac{1}{4}$ IN)

6 MM
($\frac{1}{4}$ IN)

FRONT

BACK

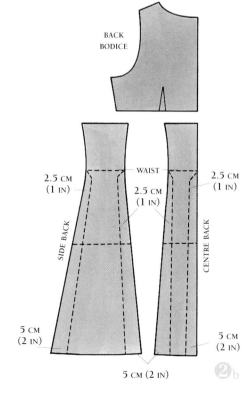

BACK
BODICE

2.5 CM
(1 IN)

WAIST

2.5 CM
(1 IN)

2.5 CM
(1 IN)

SIDE BACK

CENTRE BACK

5 CM
(2 IN)

5 CM
(2 IN)

5 CM (2 IN)

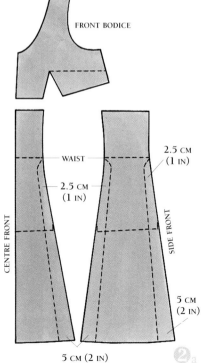

STEP 3

- Drop the bust point on the bodice about 3 cm (about 1¼ in).
- Then slash and spread the skirt panels evenly to the desired width.
- Add 1.5 cm (⅝ in) seam to the back for the zip.
- Notch the zip about 18 cm to 20 cm (about 7 in to 8 in) below the waistline.
- Add 1 cm (⅜ in) all round to the balance of the edges including the bust dart (because the bust dart is cut out as illustrated).
- Add 1 cm to 3 cm (⅜ in to about 1¼ in) for the hem.
- Notch the panels and seams carefully with the corresponding notches.
- Make the facings as illustrated, 5 cm (2 in) finished at CF and the side seams and 15 cm (6 in) at CB. Cut the centre front bodice, facing and skirt on the fold.

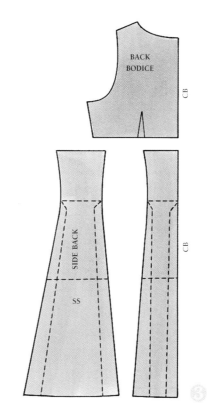

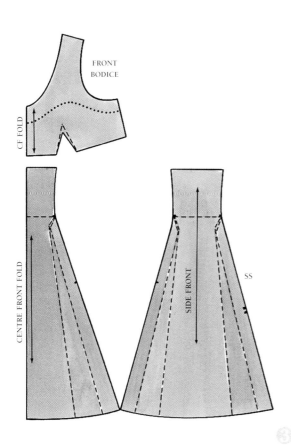

THE BODY OF THIS DRESS HAS BEEN TUCKED ON TO THE EMPIRE LINE

Dresses

A

PRINCESS LINE

The princess line resembles the panelled bodice continuing past the waistline, either with a flattering flaring skirt or a straighter shape. It may either run straight to the shoulder or curve to the armhole.

- Using the hip length foundation, follow Steps 1 and 2 on page 38.
- For Style B, extend the pattern from the hip to the desired length, keeping the panels parallel to the centre front and back.
- For Style A, extend the pattern from the waist to the desired length, adding extra fullness at the hem for flare.
- Cut the centre front on the fold.
- Add 1 cm ($\frac{3}{8}$ in) seams all round except for the centre back which should be 1.5 cm ($\frac{5}{8}$ in).
- Notch zip 18 cm to 20 cm (about 7 in to 8 in) below the waistline.
- The hem may be 1 cm to 3 cm ($\frac{3}{8}$ in to about $1\frac{1}{4}$ in), depending on the fullness of the dress. Make the appropriate notches.
- Make the facings to finish off at 5 cm (2 in) as illustrated.

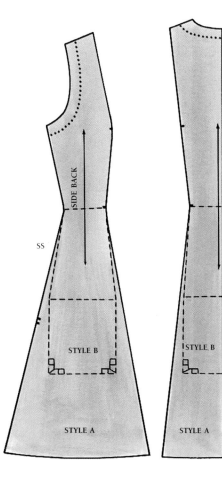

B

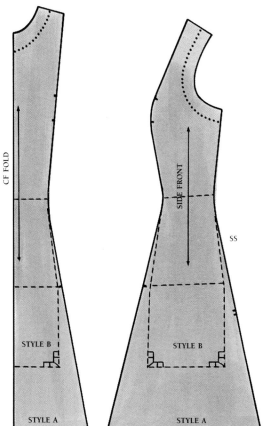

CF FOLD	SIDE FRONT	SIDE BACK	CB FOLD
	SS	SS	
STYLE B	STYLE B	STYLE B	STYLE B
STYLE A	STYLE A	STYLE A	STYLE A

NOTE

THE CENTRE BACK ZIP SHOULD END ROUGHLY 18 CM TO 20 CM (7 IN TO 8 IN) BELOW THE WAISTLINE.

COMBINING DETAILS

These styles are created by combining various bodice and skirt details. Ensure that the bodice and skirt waists correspond after gathering, darting, tucking or when easing replaces the waist dart.

PEASANT

BODICE

- See page 48 for off-the-shoulder frilled neck.
- Extend the bodice by 18 cm (about 7 in) to the hipline, eliminating the waist darts.
- Mark the waistline for the elastic positioning.
- Straighten the side seams.

SKIRT

- See page 91 for the dirndl skirt with a basque.
- Exclude the basque (already added on to the bodice).
- Add the frill to the hem, width as desired and length 2 to 3 times the hem circumference.
- Add 1 cm (⅜ in) seams all round, including hems.

SHIRTWAISTER

BODICE

- See the notched collar on page 54.
- Eliminate the waist dart, easing the bodice on to the skirt.

SKIRT

- See page 89 for the 6-gored skirt with pleats. Place CB on the fold.
- Eliminate the pleat facing to make a knife pleat instead of the inverted pleat.
- Add a buttonstand to the centre front to match that of the bodice facing.

SLEEVE

- See the shirt sleeve with cuff on page 62.
- Add 1 cm (⅜ in) seams all round. The hem may be about 3 cm (about 1¼ in).

HALTER NECK

BODICE

- See the halter neck on page 50.

SKIRT

- Refer to the full circle skirt on page 92.
- Place the side seams on the fold instead of CF and CB, so that there is a CB seam for the zip.
- Add 1 cm (⅜ in) seams to all edges, excepting the hem which should be 6 mm (¼ in).
- Notch the zip length on the skirt so that it measures 18 cm to 20 cm (about 7 in to 8 in) below the waistline.
- The full circle skirt may be replaced with the half or three-quarter circle skirt, depending on the amount of fabric available.

T r o u s e r s

Tailored trousers, track pants, or even walking shorts, are worn

by most of us because they are practical and comfortable. Use

your own basic patterns, to be sure of a good fit. To achieve

a bell-bottom shape, simply flare the legs evenly on both

sides from the knee down to the hem. Jodhpurs are widened

on the outside leg at the thigh and tightened from the knee

to the ankle. When cutting striped or checked fabrics, it is important to

ensure that the grainline is perpendicular to the hem of the trousers and,

if possible, to match the checks on the outside seams. Side seams may even

be cut on the fold, placing a dart at the waist for shaping.

PLEATED TROUSERS

Tailored trousers with pleats at the waist are elegant and flattering. To ensure a flat fit over the tummy, we extend the pocket and its facings through to the fly to hold the pleats in place.

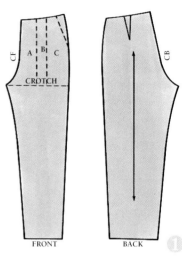

STEP 1

- Use basic trouser back as it is.
- Add 1 cm (³⁄₈ in) seams all round except at the hem, which should be 2 cm (³⁄₄ in).
- Trace the outline of the trouser front.
- Establish the position of the pocket (opening to be a minimum of 15 cm [6 in]) and position the tucks.
- Mark the crotch line, then the vertical lines from the tuck points to the crotch line, as illustrated.

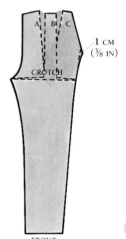

STEP 2

- Slash the vertical lines from the waist down to the crotch line, then across to the crotch point and the side seam respectively, ensuring that all the pieces still remain attached.
- Spread the tucks to the desired width, extend the pocket opening by 1 cm (³⁄₈ in), curving the side seam to that point.
- This prevents the pocket from pulling too tightly over the hip when it is stitched.

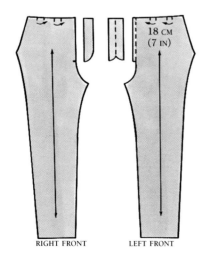

RIGHT FRONT   LEFT FRONT

STEP 3

- Trim the panels A and C at the waist to match panel B and mark the tucks.
- Make the right front pattern by copying the left front.
- On the left front, add 1 cm (³⁄₈ in) to the centre front crotch from the waist to the 18 cm (7 in) mark (for an 18 cm or 7 in zip). This extra 1 cm (³⁄₈ in) ensures that the zip is not exposed to the eye.
- Extend to 20 cm (8 in) for a longer zip.
- Add 1 cm (³⁄₈ in) seams; the hem being 2 cm (³⁄₄ in).

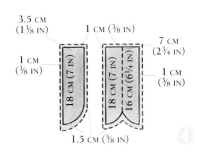

STEP 4

- Make the placket for the attachment to the left front as illustrated: 7 cm by 18 cm (2¼ in by 7 in) (for 18 cm or 7 in zip) curving up to 16 cm (6¼ in) in the centre at the bottom. When adding the seams, add 1 cm (⅜ in) to the top and sides but 1.5 cm (⅝ in) to the curved bottom.
- For fly facing: 3.5 cm by 18 cm (1⅜ in by 7 in) curving up to about 16 cm (6¼ in) on one side. Add 1 cm (⅜ in) seam to the top and straight side, and 1.5 cm (⅝ in) to the curved side, as illustrated. The fly facing is attached to the right front.

STEP 5

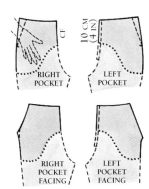

- Use the fitted trouser front (not the pleated front) to make the pockets. The side seam should be about 25 cm (about 10 in) in length and the centre front about 10 cm (4 in).
- To mark the pocket opening, place your hand on the pattern, as illustrated, and mark the S-shaped bottom of the pocket from the centre front (CF) to the side seam around the hand.
- Make right and left pocket pieces, adding 1 cm (⅜ in) on to the left centre front to correspond with the pleated pattern.

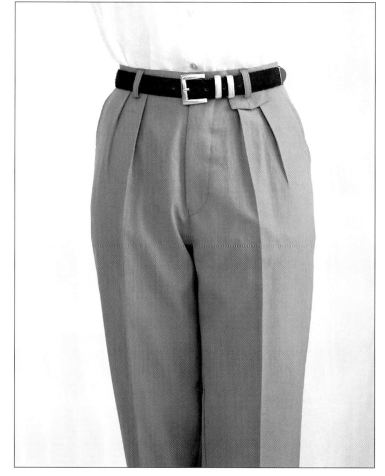

PLEATED TROUSERS CAN HAVE A SLIMMING EFFECT

H A N D Y   H I N T S

USE THESE POCKET PATTERNS TO MAKE THE POCKET FACINGS. THE POCKET OPENING SHOULD CORRESPOND WITH THE PLEATED FRONTS. ADD 1 CM (⅜ IN) SEAMS. FOR THE WAISTBAND SEE PAGE 86.

Trousers

JEANS

Denim jeans are probably the most popular style ever to be created. The fabric, serge, originated in Nîmes, France, and the style was first used for overalls by workers. Today the leg shape varies with fashion trends but the overall style remains the same.

STEP 1

- Trace the outline of the front and back of the trousers.
- Establish the front pocket position (an opening of at least 15 cm or 6 in) and back yoke.
- Trim down the inner and outer seams, as desired, for slim jeans.

SLIM-FITTING JEANS

COWBOY JEANS

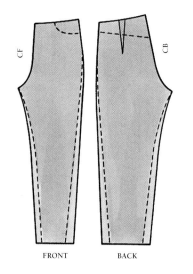

FRONT   BACK

1 CM (³⁄₈ IN)   1 CM (³⁄₈ IN)

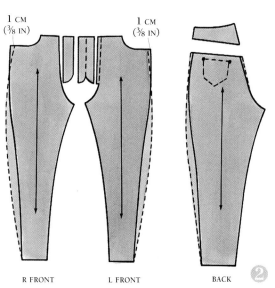

R FRONT   L FRONT   BACK

STEP 2

- Trace the right and left front with the new shape.
- Extend the pocket openings by 1 cm (³⁄₈ in), easing off on to the side seams.
- Add 1 cm (³⁄₈ in) to the centre front (CF) of the left front from the waist 18 cm to 20 cm (7 in to 8 in) down, as on the pleated trousers.
- Add 1 cm (³⁄₈ in) seams, the hem being 2 cm (³⁄₄ in).
- Cut through the yoke at the back and close the dart.
- Eliminate the remainder of the dart on the back by trimming off the side seam and the centre back (CB) seam to the corresponding measurements of the yoke.
- Add 1 cm (³⁄₈ in) seams, and a 2 cm (³⁄₄ in) hem.
  For the fly facing and placket construction, follow the instructions given for the pleated trousers in Step 4.
- For the cowboy jeans, alter the leg shape as indicated by the dotted line.

STEP 3

- Use the basic front to make the right and left pockets. The side seam should be about 22 cm (about 8¾ in) and the centre front length about 10 cm (4 in).
- Mark the pocket opening.
- Curve the bottom of the pocket as illustrated.
- Add 1 cm (⅜ in) to the left front crotch to correspond with the left front leg.
- Make right and left pocket facings from these, ensuring that the opening corresponds with the trouser patterns.
- Add 1 cm (⅜ in) seams all round and notch appropriately.
- Make the back patch pockets as illustrated: 16 cm (6¼ in) across at the opening by 13 cm (about 5¼ in) in length at the sides and 16 cm (6¼ in) in the centre and by 14 cm (5½ in) across at the bottom, as illustrated.
- Centre the pocket length by 16 cm (6¼ in).
- Add a 2 cm (¾ in) hem and 1 cm (⅜ in) to the balance of the seams.
- Mark pocket position on back trouser panel.
- See page 86 for the waistband.
- Make the belt loops to measure 1 cm (⅜ in) in width when finished.

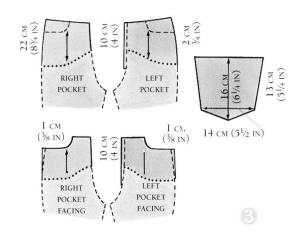

H A N D Y   H I N T S

To eliminate bulkiness across the tummy, especially when using denim fabric, use calico for the pocket facings.

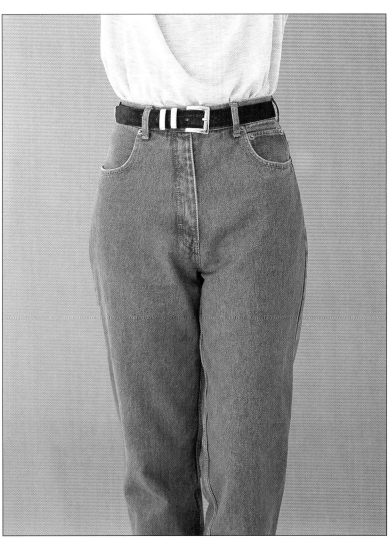

REGULAR-FIT JEANS

Trousers

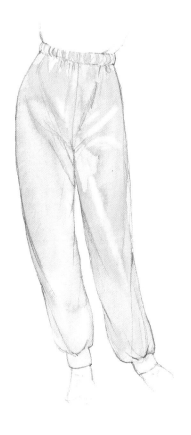

TRACK PANTS

Track pants are probably the most comfortable trousers one can wear. Although not often flattering, they are very practical for various occasions.

WITHOUT SIDE SEAMS

- Trace the front and back pants with the side seams touching.
- Taper the inside legs as desired and shorten the length to accommodate the rib or add to the length for elasticating the hem.
- Establish the width of the waist elastic and add twice this measurement to the centre front and the centre back crotch. Draw a straight line from the centre front to the centre back, as illustrated.
- Add 1 cm (³⁄₈ in) seams all round.
- For grainline, fold pattern in half, matching the seams at the hem and the crotch.

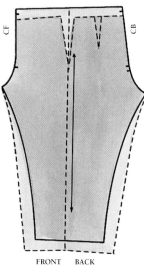

FRONT   BACK

WITH SIDE SEAMS

- Trace the front and back separately.
- Taper the legs as desired and shorten the leg for the rib or lengthen for the elastic.
- Straighten the side seams from the hip upwards.
- Establish the waist elastic width and lengthen the front and back crotch as well as the side seams by twice this amount.
- Add 1 cm (³⁄₈ in) seams all round.
- Draw a grainline in the centre of each panel.

- The length of the cuff will depend on the elasticity of the ribbing used.
- The ribbing must be cut on the fold to the desired width.
- Add 1 cm (³⁄₈ in) seams.

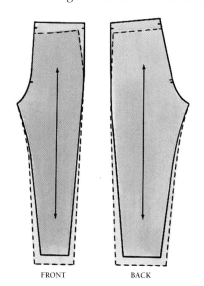

FRONT   BACK

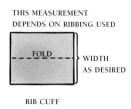

THIS MEASUREMENT
DEPENDS ON RIBBING USED

FOLD   WIDTH
AS DESIRED

RIB CUFF

HANDY HINTS

As track pants are usually cut in knitted fleece, they tend to bag at the knee. To avoid this, add more fullness to the pattern. The looser the fit, the less likely it is to stretch out. Ribbing with lycra thread has more elasticity and will therefore grip better.

RUNNING SHORTS

Running shorts or other short shorts should fit comfortably across the thigh without causing constriction. When choosing the length, ensure that the shorts do not end at an unattractive point on your leg.

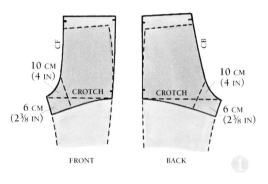

STEP 1

- Trace the outline of the front and back slim trousers.
- Establish the width of the waist elastic and lengthen the front and back crotch and side seams by twice this amount.
- Straighten the side seam upwards at the same time.
- Mark the inside leg 6 cm (2⅜ in) down from the crotch and draw a curved line to the crotch line at the side seam on both the front and the back.

STEP 2

- The thigh may be reduced by slashing the dotted line from the edge to the crotch and overlapping it by about 1.25 cm (½ in) or as desired. Add 1 cm (⅜ in) for the seams and the hem.
- Notch the fold line at the waist and 4 cm (1½ in) side slits.

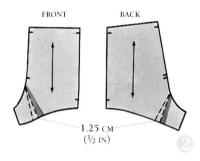

WALKING SHORTS

Walking shorts are smart and tailored, with waist tucks. They are usually cut to knee-length and may be worn in summer or in winter depending on the fabric used.

STEP 1

- Establish the length of the shorts and the hem circumference.
  Trace the front and back trousers to the shorts length, and alter the width as desired.
- Mark the pocket and slash the lines for the tucks.
- Add 1 cm (⅜ in) seams and a 2 cm (¾ in) hem to the back.

STEP 2

- Slash the tuck lines from the waist to the hem, ensuring that all the pieces remain attached.
- Spread the tucks to the desired width.
- Continue by following the rest of Step 2 of the Pleated Trousers on page 104 and continuing to the end of the construction.

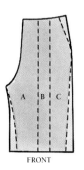

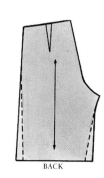

Trousers

CHAPTER XII

Quarter-Scale Patterns

These patterns have been based on the standard body measurements and when scaled up. may be altered to your specific measurements or may be used as is. This task is not quite as daunting as it at first appears. The necessary ease required for each pattern is included. No seams or hems have been included and should be added on completion of the pattern-making. Please bear this in mind if you use these patterns for further styling.

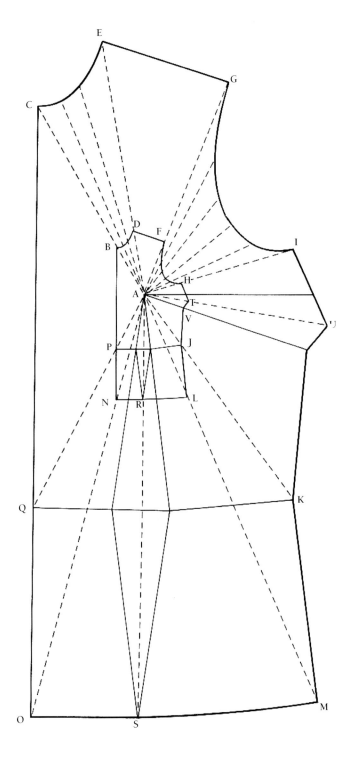

BODICE

Trace the outline of the front.
Mark the scale lines from the bust point
A through various points on the outline
as illustrated.

Scale as follows

AC = 4 x AB
AE = 4 x AD
AG = 4 x AF
AI = 4 x AH
AK = 4 x AJ
AM = 4 x AL
AO = 4 x AN
AQ = 4 x AP

Divide the neck into 3 or 4 equal parts.
Draw the scale lines from A through the dividing
points, making the line four times the length of
the original line.
Divide the armhole into 5 or 6 equal parts.
Draw the scale lines and extend as for the neck.
Draw the scale line through the centre of the dart.

AS = 4 x AR
AU = 4 x AT
AW = 4 x AV

Connect all the points to form a new outline.
Mark the waistline QK.
Extend the vertical dart to the new
waistline and then to S.
Extend the bust dart to the new outline.
Use this method to scale up all the fronts and backs
of all the bodices, blouses, dresses and jackets.
Similarly scale up the sleeve, trousers and skirt
marking scale lines as illustrated.
From the centre point each line must be extended
by 4 times the original amount.

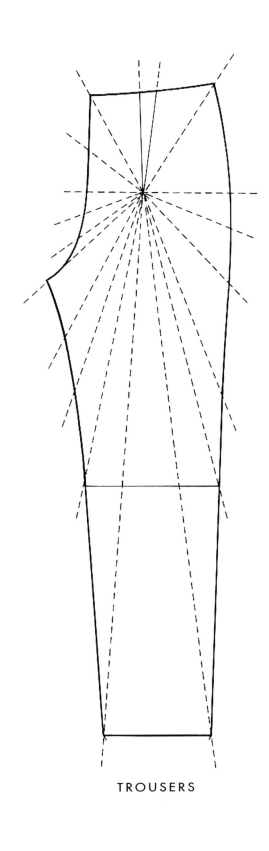

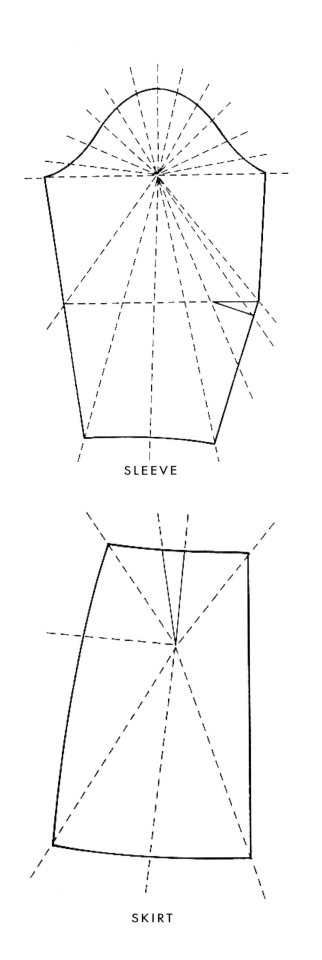

SLEEVE

SKIRT

TROUSERS

Scaling Patterns

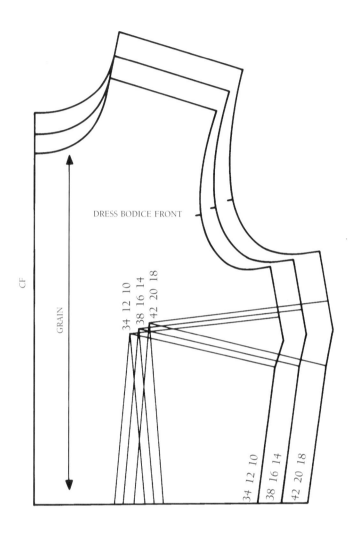

DRESS BODICE FRONT

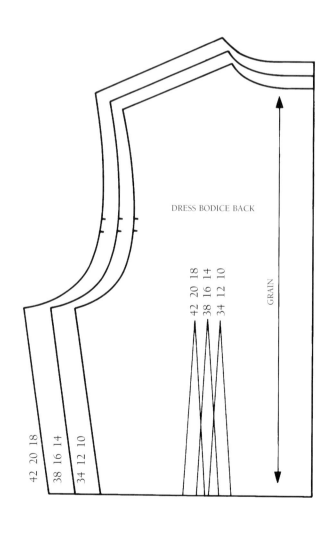

DRESS BODICE BACK

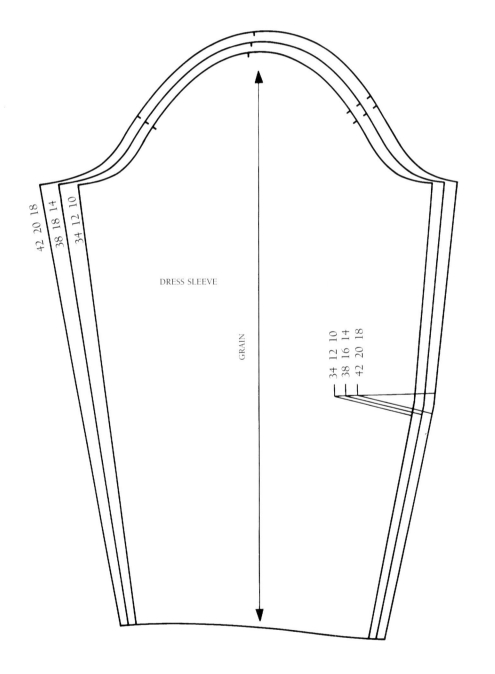

DRESS SLEEVE

GRAIN

42 20 18
38 18 14
34 12 10

34 12 10
38 16 14
42 20 18

DRESS SLEEVE

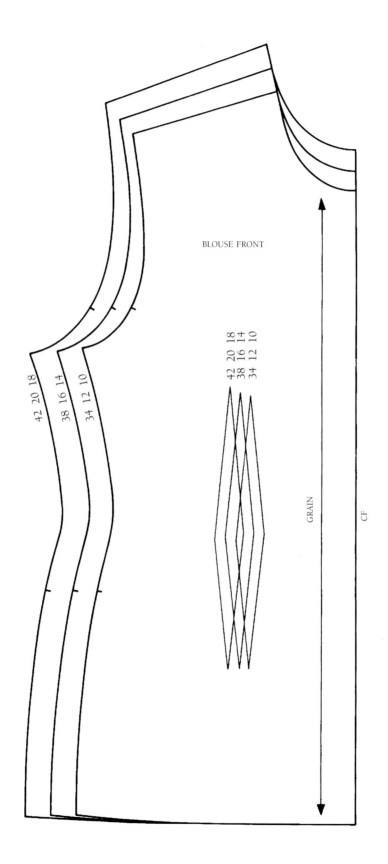

BLOUSE FRONT

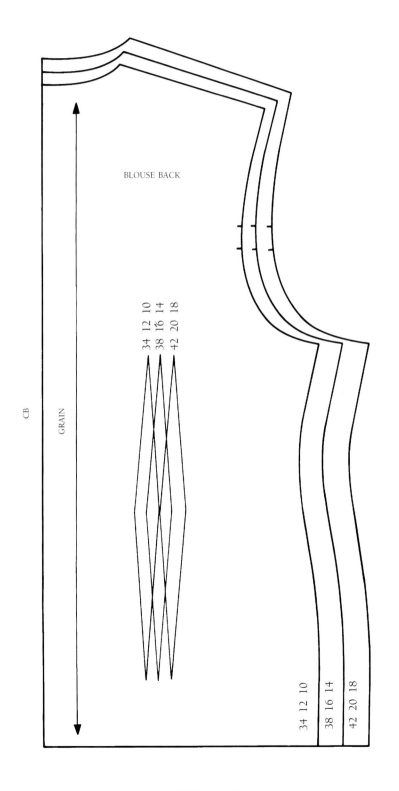

BLOUSE BACK

BLOUSE BACK

CB

GRAIN

34 12 10
38 16 14
42 20 18

34 12 10
38 16 14
42 20 18

Scaling Patterns

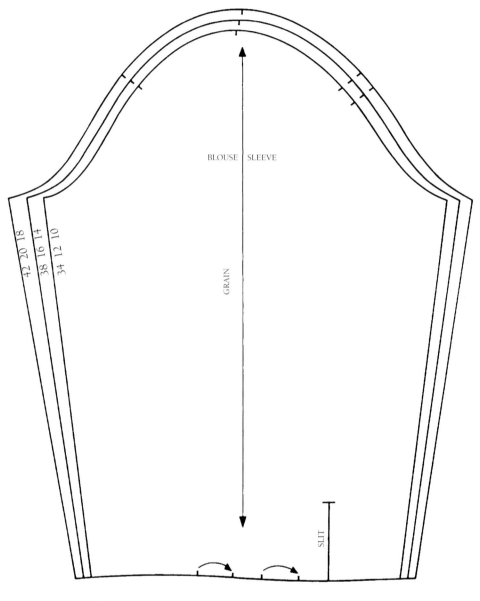

BLOUSE SLEEVE

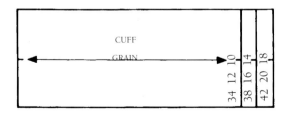

CUFF

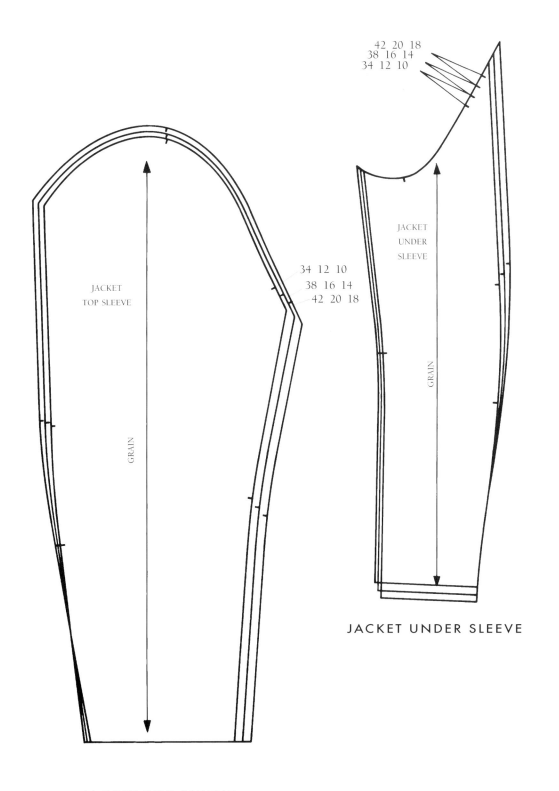

42 20 18
38 16 14
34 12 10

JACKET
UNDER
SLEEVE

34 12 10
38 16 14
42 20 18

JACKET
TOP SLEEVE

GRAIN

GRAIN

JACKET UNDER SLEEVE

JACKET TOP SLEEVE

Scaling Patterns

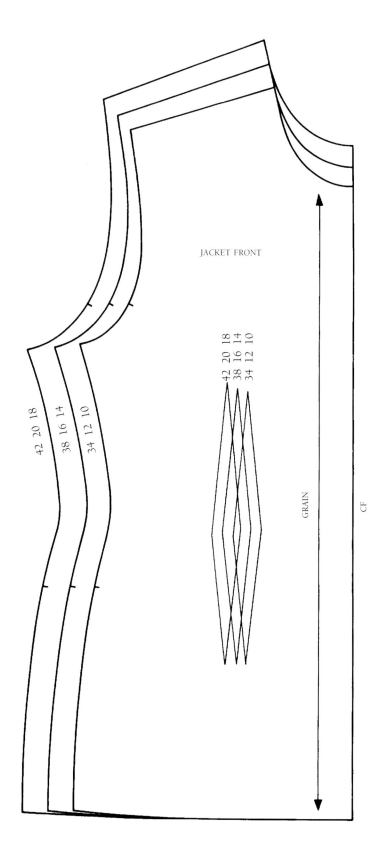

42 20 18
38 16 14
34 12 10

JACKET FRONT

42 20 18
38 16 14
34 12 10

GRAIN

CF

JACKET FRONT

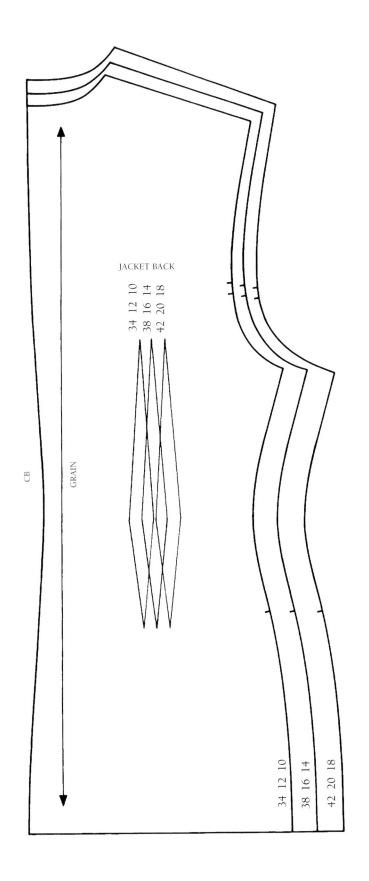

CB

GRAIN

JACKET BACK

34 12 10
38 16 14
42 20 18

34 12 10
38 16 14
42 20 18

JACKET BACK

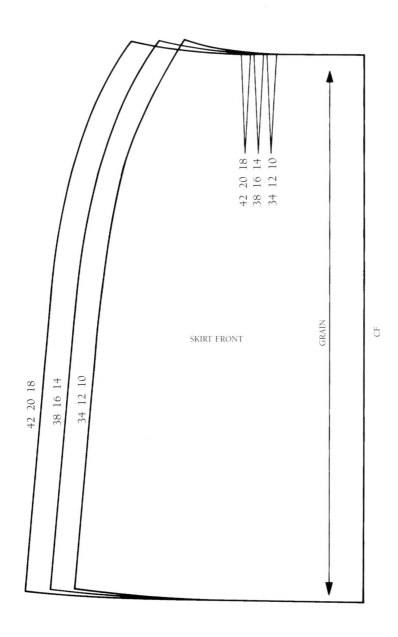

SKIRT FRONT

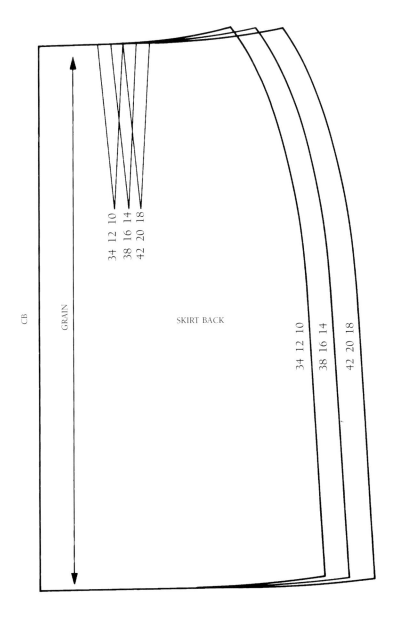

SKIRT BACK

Scaling Patterns

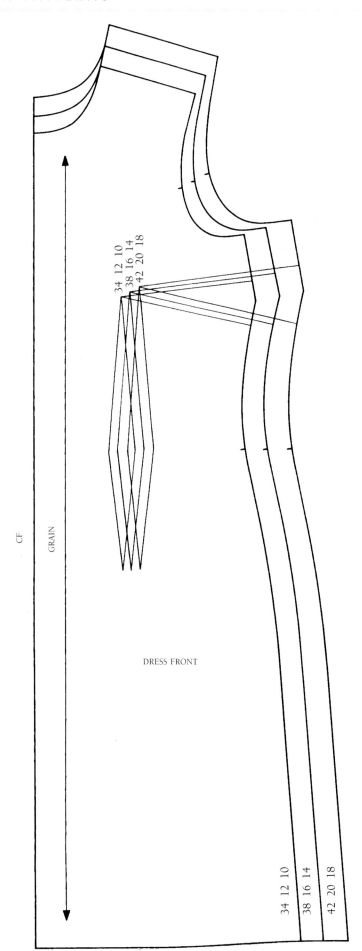

DRESS FRONT

CF

GRAIN

34 12 10
38 16 14
42 20 18

DRESS FRONT

34 12 10

38 16 14

42 20 18

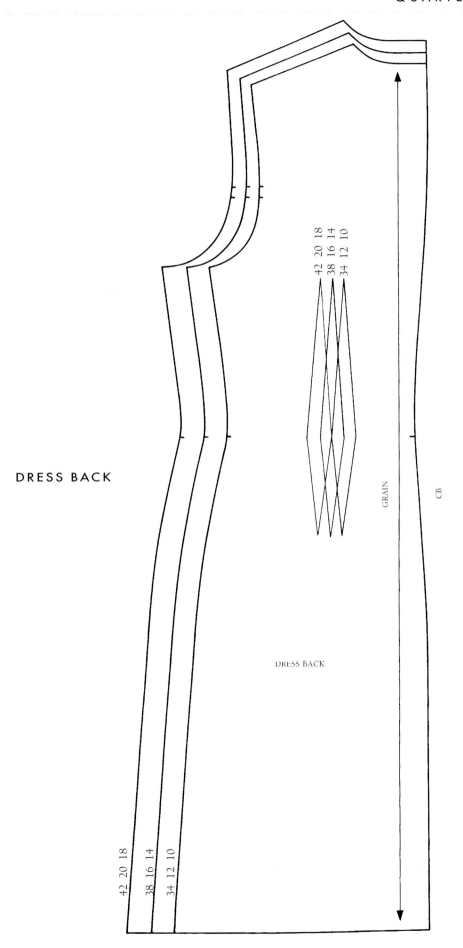

DRESS BACK

42 20 18
38 16 14
34 12 10

GRAIN

CB

DRESS BACK

42 20 18
38 16 14
34 12 10

Scaling Patterns

125

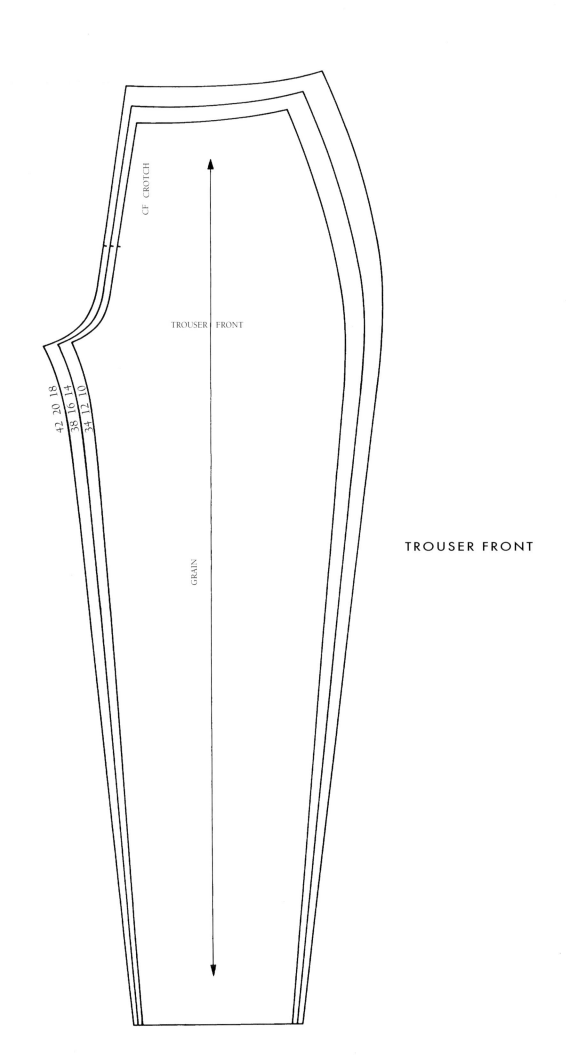

CF CROTCH

TROUSER FRONT

42 20 18
38 16 14
34 12 10

GRAIN

TROUSER FRONT

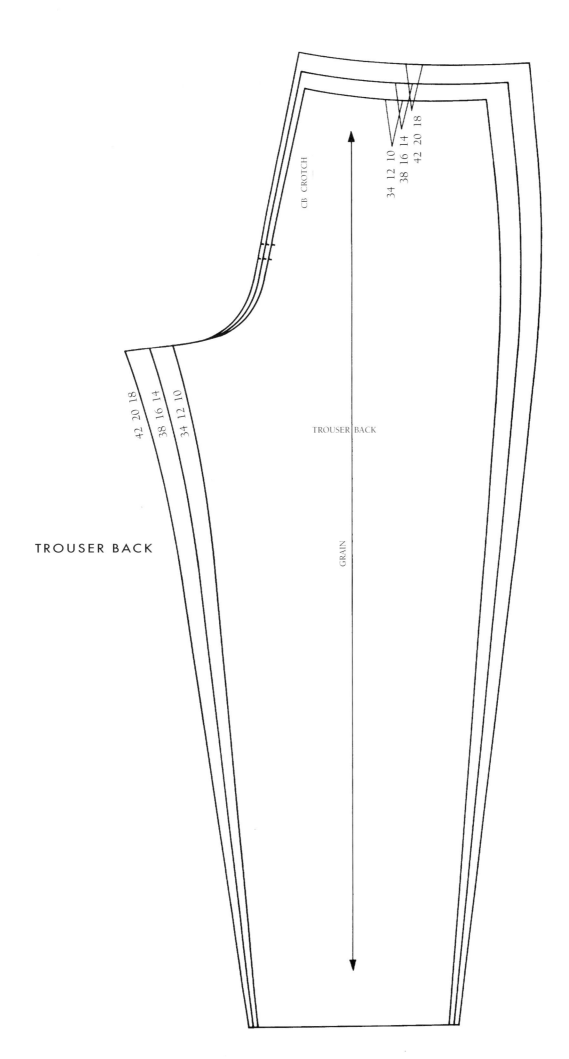

CB CROTCH

34 12 10
38 16 14
42 20 18

42 20 18
38 16 14
34 12 10

TROUSER BACK

GRAIN

TROUSER BACK

Index